THE
CHIPEWYAN

THE
CHIPEWYAN

Kim Dramer

Frank W. Porter III
General Editor

CHELSEA HOUSE PUBLISHERS
New York Philadelphia

On the cover   A pair of beaded smoked moose-hide moccasins, made in 1972 by Maria Houle, a Chipewyan-Cree Métis artist from Fort Chipewyan, Alberta.

Chelsea House Publishers
Editorial Director   Richard Rennert
Executive Managing Editor   Karyn Gullen Browne
Copy Chief   Robin James
Picture Editor   Adrian G. Allen
Creative Director   Robert Mitchell
Art Director   Joan Ferrigno
Production Manager   Sallye Scott

Indians of North America
Senior Editor   Sean Dolan
Native American Specialist   Jack Miller

Staff for **THE CHIPEWYAN**
Associate Editor   Mary B. Sisson
Senior Designer   Cambraia Magalhães
Picture Researcher   Lisa Kirschner

First Printing

1 3 5 7 9 8 6 4 2

Library of Congress Cataloging-in-Publication Data

Dramer, Kim.
   The Chipewyan / Kim Dramer; Frank W. Porter III, general editor.
      p. cm. — (Indians of North America)
   Includes bibliographical references and index.
   Summary: Examines the history and culture of the Chipewyan, whose subarctic environment led them to a way of life taking advantage of the intense cold.
   ISBN 1-55546-139-5.
      0-7910-3480-1 (pbk.)
   1. Chipewyan Indians—History—Juvenile literature.
2. Chipewyan Indians—Social life and customs—Juvenile literature.
[1. Chipewyan Indians. 2. Indians of North America—Canada.]
I. Porter, Frank W., 1947–   . II. Title. III. Series: Indians of North America (Chelsea House Publishers)
E99.C59D73 1995   95-3532
971'.004972—dc20   CIP
                                                AC

CONTENTS

INDIANS OF NORTH AMERICA

CHELSEA HOUSE PUBLISHERS

INDIANS OF NORTH AMERICA: CONFLICT AND SURVIVAL

Frank W. Porter III

The Indians survived our open intention of wiping them out, and since the tide turned they have even weathered our good intentions toward them, which can be much more deadly.

John Steinbeck
America and Americans

When Europeans first reached the North American continent, they found hundreds of tribes occupying a vast and rich country. The newcomers quickly recognized the wealth of natural resources. They were not, however, so quick or willing to recognize the spiritual, cultural, and intellectual riches of the people they called Indians.

The Indians of North America examines the problems that develop when people with different cultures come together. For American Indians, the consequences of their interaction with non-Indian people have been both productive and tragic. The Europeans believed they had "discovered" a "New World," but their religious bigotry, cultural bias, and materialistic world view kept them from appreciating and understanding the people who lived in it. All too often they attempted to change the way of life of the indigenous people. The Spanish conquistadores wanted the Indians as a source of labor. The Christian missionaries, many of whom were English, viewed them as potential converts. French traders and trappers used the Indians as a means to obtain pelts. As Francis Parkman, the 19th-century historian, stated, "Spanish civilization crushed the Indian; English civilization scorned and neglected him. French civilization embraced and cherished him."

Nearly 500 years later, many people think of American Indians as curious vestiges of a distant past, waging a futile war to survive in a Space Age society. Even today, our understanding of the history and culture of American Indians is too often derived from unsympathetic, culturally biased, and inaccurate reports. The American Indian, described and portrayed in thousands of movies, television programs, books, articles, and government studies, has either been raised to the status of the "noble savage" or disparaged as the "wild Indian" who resisted the westward expansion of the American frontier.

Where in this popular view are the real Indians, the human beings and communities whose ancestors can be traced back to ice-age hunters? Where are the creative and indomitable people whose sophisticated technologies used the natural resources to ensure their survival, whose military skill might even have prevented European settlement of North America if not for devastating epidemics and disruption of the ecology? Where are the men and women who are today diligently struggling to assert their legal rights and express once again the value of their heritage?

The various Indian tribes of North America, like people everywhere, have a history that includes population expansion, adaptation to a range of regional environments, trade across wide networks, internal strife, and warfare. This was the reality. Europeans justified their conquests, however, by creating a mythical image of the New World and its native people. In this myth, the New World was a virgin land, waiting for the Europeans. The arrival of Christopher Columbus ended a timeless primitiveness for the original inhabitants.

Also part of this myth was the debate over the origins of the American Indians. Fantastic and diverse answers were proposed by the early explorers, missionaries, and settlers. Some thought that the Indians were descended from the Ten Lost Tribes of Israel, others that they were descended from inhabitants of the lost continent of Atlantis. One writer suggested that the Indians had reached North America in another Noah's ark.

A later myth, perpetrated by many historians, focused on the relentless persecution during the past five centuries until only a scattering of these "primitive" people remained to be herded onto reservations. This view fails to chronicle the overt and covert ways in which the Indians successfully coped with the intruders.

All of these myths presented one-sided interpretations that ignored the complexity of European and American events and policies. All left serious questions unanswered. What were the origins of the American Indians? Where did they come from? How and when did they get to the New World? What was their life—their culture—really like?

In the late 1800s, anthropologists and archaeologists in the Smithsonian Institution's newly created Bureau of American Ethnology in Washington, D.C., began to study scientifically the history and culture of the Indians of North

America. They were motivated by an honest belief that the Indians were on the verge of extinction and that along with them would vanish their languages, religious beliefs, technology, myths, and legends. These men and women went out to visit, study, and record data from as many Indian communities as possible before this information was forever lost.

By this time there was a new myth in the national consciousness. American Indians existed as figures in the American past. They had performed a historical mission. They had challenged white settlers who trekked across the continent. Once conquered, however, they were supposed to accept graciously the way of life of their conquerors.

The reality again was different. American Indians resisted both actively and passively. They refused to lose their unique identity, to be assimilated into white society. Many whites viewed the Indians not only as members of a conquered nation but also as "inferior" and "unequal." The rights of the Indians could be expanded, contracted, or modified as the conquerors saw fit. In every generation, white society asked itself what to do with the American Indians. Their answers have resulted in the twists and turns of federal Indian policy.

There were two general approaches. One way was to raise the Indians to a "higher level" by "civilizing" them. Zealous missionaries considered it their Christian duty to elevate the Indian through conversion and scanty education. The other approach was to ignore the Indians until they disappeared under pressure from the ever-expanding white society. The myth of the "vanishing Indian" gave stronger support to the latter option, helping to justify the taking of the Indians' land.

Prior to the end of the 18th century, there was no national policy on Indians simply because the American nation had not yet come into existence. American Indians similarly did not possess a political or social unity with which to confront the various Europeans. They were not homogeneous. Rather, they were loosely formed bands and tribes, speaking nearly 300 languages and thousands of dialects. The collective identity felt by Indians today is a result of their common experiences of defeat and/or mistreatment at the hands of whites.

During the colonial period, the British crown did not have a coordinated policy toward the Indians of North America. Specific tribes (most notably the Iroquois and the Cherokee) became military and political pawns used by both the crown and the individual colonies. The success of the American Revolution brought no immediate change. When the United States acquired new territory from France and Mexico in the early 19th century, the federal government wanted to open this land to settlement by homesteaders. But the Indian tribes that lived on this land had signed treaties with European governments assuring their title to the land. Now the United States assumed legal responsibility for honoring these treaties.

At first, President Thomas Jefferson believed that the Louisiana Purchase contained sufficient land for both the Indians and the white population. Within a generation, though, it became clear that the Indians would not be allowed to remain. In the 1830s the federal government began to coerce the eastern tribes to sign treaties agreeing to relinquish their ancestral land and move west of the Mississippi River. Whenever these negotiations failed, President Andrew Jackson used the military to remove the Indians. The southeastern tribes, promised food and transportation during their removal to the West, were instead forced to walk the "Trail of Tears." More than 4,000 men, woman, and children died during this forced march. The "removal policy" was successful in opening the land to homesteaders, but it created enormous hardships for the Indians.

By 1871 most of the tribes in the United States had signed treaties ceding most or all of their ancestral land in exchange for reservations and welfare. The treaty terms were intended to bind both parties for all time. But in the General Allotment Act of 1887, the federal government changed its policy again. Now the goal was to make tribal members into individual landowners and farmers, encouraging their absorption into white society. This policy was advantageous to whites who were eager to acquire Indian land, but it proved disastrous for the Indians. One hundred thirty-eight million acres of reservation land were subdivided into tracts of 160, 80, or as little as 40 acres, and allotted tribe members on an individual basis. Land owned in this way was said to have "trust status" and could not be sold. But the surplus land—all Indian land not allotted to individuals—was opened (for sale) to white settlers. Ultimately, more than 90 million acres of land were taken from the Indians by legal and illegal means.

The resulting loss of land was a catastrophe for the Indians. It was necessary to make it illegal for Indians to sell their land to non-Indians. The Indian Reorganization Act of 1934 officially ended the allotment period. Tribes that voted to accept the provisions of this act were reorganized, and an effort was made to purchase land within preexisting reservations to restore an adequate land base.

Ten years later, in 1944, federal Indian policy again shifted. Now the federal government wanted to get out of the "Indian business." In 1953 an act of Congress named specific tribes whose trust status was to be ended "at the earliest possible time." This new law enabled the United States to end unilaterally, whether the Indians wished it or not, the special status that protected the land in Indian tribal reservations. In the 1950s federal Indian policy was to transfer federal responsibility and jurisdiction to state governments, encourage the physical relocation of Indian peoples from reservations to urban areas, and hasten the termination, or extinction, of tribes.

Between 1954 and 1962 Congress passed specific laws authorizing the termination of more than 100 tribal groups. The stated purpose of the termination policy was to ensure the full and complete integration of Indians into American society. However, there is a less benign way to interpret this legislation. Even as termination was being discussed in Congress, 133 separate bills were introduced to permit the transfer of trust land ownership from Indians to non-Indians.

With the Johnson administration in the 1960s the federal government began to reject termination. In the 1970s yet another Indian policy emerged. Known as "self-determination," it favored keeping the protective role of the federal government while increasing tribal participation in, and control of, important areas of local government. In 1983 President Reagan, in a policy statement on Indian affairs, restated the unique "government is government" relationship of the United States with the Indians. However, federal programs since then have moved toward transferring Indian affairs to individual states, which have long desired to gain control of Indian land and resources.

As long as American Indians retain power, land, and resources that are coveted by the states and the federal government, there will continue to be a "clash of cultures," and the issues will be contested in the courts, Congress, the White House, and even in the international human rights community. To give all Americans a greater comprehension of the issues and conflicts involving American Indians today is a major goal of this series. These issues are not easily understood, nor can these conflicts be readily resolved. The study of North American Indian history and culture is a necessary and important step toward that comprehension. All Americans must learn the history of the relations between the Indians and the federal government, recognize the unique legal status of the Indians, and understand the heritage and cultures of the Indians of North America.

"The land of little sticks," the traditional home of the Chipewyans, is a band of thinning forest located in northern Canada. The area is a transitional region between the tundra to the north and the thick forests to the south.

CARIBOU HUNTERS

The Great White North of Canada is a vast region. Almost half the size of the United States, it is populated by less than one person per 100 square miles. Frozen for most of the year beneath ice and snow, it seems an inhospitable environment where few people would dare to live in defiance of nature's cold hand. Yet for those who know the land, it is a place of great bounty, rich resources, and secure livelihood. Such people are the Chipewyans.

The Chipewyans live in the forest-tundra ecotone, a narrow zone of thinning forest (called taiga) between the sweeping tundra bordering the Arctic Ocean to the north and the forest of conifer and hardy deciduous trees to the south. Known as "the land of little sticks" due to the limitations of growth caused by arctic winds from the north, this belt of transitional forest is rarely more than 100 miles in width. Within these narrow borders the Chipewyans carried on their traditional way of life for millennia, living as hunter-gatherers. Exploiting the subarctic land for their existence, the Chipewyans developed a rich civilization that is a masterpiece of adaptive strategies and cultural flexibility.

Instead of attempting to defy the cold, the Chipewyans created a way of life that relied on it. Intense cold made hunting easier for the knowledgeable Chipewyans. Freezing arctic winds from the north caused moose to seek wintering grounds in the shelter of valleys, where they were easily ambushed by Chipewyan hunters. The snow held tracks of rabbits and other small animals, revealing to Chipewyan women the best places to set snares. Trees lost their leaves, making the grouse that gathered on low branches easy targets for Chipewyan arrows. When the lakes froze, the fish became slower and easier to catch in the rawhide or willow-bark nets that Chipewyan fishermen lowered through holes chipped

A late-19th-century Chipewyan dog sled and team, photographed outside of Fort Chipewyan in present-day Alberta.

through the ice with horn chisels. Travel was easier in winter; the Chipewyans used special toboggans or sledges made of pierced caribou leg skins that slid easily over the frozen ground and were better suited to trails running through terrain with trees and tree stumps than the sleds with runners used by their Inuit neighbors to the north.

Chipewyan life was so suited to the cold that the yearly thaw, rather than the bitter winter, was the time of the most

danger and uncertainty. The territory of the Chipewyans was awash with lakes and marshes that could be speedily crossed with sledges when frozen; when the thaw came, however, the water made sledge travel impractical. Melting snow made the ground marshy so that it did not hold the tracks of animals well. In addition, wet ground made the Chipewyans more susceptible to frostbite and hypothermia because their leather moccasins and clothing would soak up the moisture and retain cold. This problem was so serious that Chipewyan hunters would often strip off their moccasins and walk barefoot during the daytime in order to keep their footgear dry for the colder night.

Summer was a somewhat easier time, because the Chipewyans could abandon their nomadic pursuit of game and settle into summer fishing camps by the northern lakes. Chipewyans fished for pike, trout, and whitefish, which were eaten raw or smoked. The Chipewyans abandoned sledges altogether during the warm weather, traveling on foot or by canoes made of hide or spruce and birch bark collected in the spring when the sap was running and the bark of the trees was easier to peel in large pieces. Usually several families would come together in the summer to engage in feasting and dancing to the music of drums, which were made from caribou hides stretched taut over frames of willow, giving a deep resonating sound when beaten with a heavy stick. Presents were usually exchanged at this time, and prospective marriage partners were sought.

The most important game animal to the Chipewyans was not fish but caribou. Indeed, the customs, material and spiritual culture, and economic and social structure of the Chipewyans were defined by their pursuit of the Barren Grounds caribou, *Rangifer tarandus groenlandicus*. The Chipewyans occupied two discrete territories, both based on the ranges of various caribou herds. The Chipewyans living directly west of Hudson Bay (called the Northern Indians by fur trad-

ers) exploited what Canadian Wildlife biologists now call the Kaminuriak and Beverly herds of caribou, while the Chipewyans living between the Great Slave and Contwoyto Lakes (called the Yellowknives or Copper Indians) exploited the Bathurst herd. The caribou structured the seasonal cycle of the Chipewyans. Every fall, to escape the intense northern cold, the caribou would migrate south in herds that sometimes numbered in the hundreds of thousands, and every spring they would travel north again to their calving grounds in the tundra. The Chipewyans migrated as well, intercepting the caribou herds on their biannual journey and killing great numbers of the animals to supply their needs.

Caribou provided meat and fat for food, skins for shelter and clothing, and horn and bone for tools. The camp lodges that provided shelter for the Chipewyan hunters and their families were made of caribou hides stretched over a framework of poles. Chipewyan hunters wore breechcloths, leggings, shirts, and moccasins made of caribou hide, which was light, supple, and warm. Caribou-skin clothing was so popular, in fact, that the Chipewyans were named after their caribou-skin shirts. The term *Chipewyan* is thought to come from a Cree word, *chipawayanawok*, meaning "pointed skins," a reference to the traditional Chipewyan caribou-skin shirts, which came to a point in the back. (The Chipewyans call themselves simply *Dene*, "the people.")

Caribou also left a mark on Chipewyan mythology. During the long winter, when the aurora borealis shines its light

Chipewyan fish camps, such as the one pictured above, were usually active in the summer. In a good season, enough fish could be caught and dried to last the entire year.

over the Arctic, the Chipewyans say it is a caribou whose skin sparkles in the winter light of the sky. According to Chipewyan oral tradition, during the time of the ancestors, man and caribou were joined forever. The ruler of all the caribou is called "the little caribou calf." His mother was human and his father was a caribou. He fled to join the kin of his father after being treated badly by his mother's people, but now, when called upon by humans, he sends the caribou to the Chipewyan camps.

Caribou travel vast distances on their annual migration, and the Chipewyans did as well. This nomadic way of life left no chance for sowing or harvesting crops, and the Chipewyans never farmed. In fact, with the exception of berries picked and eaten at the end of each summer, plants simply did not form a part of the Chipewyan diet, which was an estimated 90 percent animal tissue. Soil in the subarctic region is thin and acidic and is made even less fertile by the existence of permafrost, frozen ground a few feet below the surface that never thaws, even in summer. On the thin layer of thawed earth grow willow scrub, scattered stands of birch and spruce, and lichens and moss. This is the food upon which caribou and other grazing animals fed; upon these animals fed the Chipewyans.

The ability of the Chipewyans to live off their subarctic homeland created quite an impression on the Europeans who entered their territory and who wrote with admiration of the security the Chipewyans received from a seemingly inhospitable land. Despite what they considered their overwhelmingly superior technology, the Europeans were never able to survive in the subarctic without the help of the Chipewyans, and to this day Euro-Canadian settlements in this area tend to be temporary and to exist only by importing large amounts of supplies from further south.

The Chipewyans' ability to survive was explained by a Hudson's Bay Company explorer named Samuel Hearne, who wrote in 1771:

> As their whole aim is to procure a comfortable subsistence, they take the most prudent methods to accomplish it; and by always following the lead of the deer [caribou], are seldom exposed to the griping hand of famine, so frequently felt by those [Europeans] who are called the annual traders.

Because the Chipewyans always followed "the lead of the deer," a large element of unpredictability surrounded their living situation. A hunter and his family had to be ready to move at a moment's notice, and to make the move easier they could take only those items necessary for survival that could not be manufactured at the next campsite. The new camp might be in the taiga, the tundra, or the woods, and different strategies and equipment were needed to live in these different environments.

Because of their migratory way of life and the demands of their environment, the Chipewyans built no permanent cities with large buildings, or great libraries with books to spread their knowledge of the subarctic. For this reason, the Chipewyans were often mistaken by outsiders as an impoverished people with a primitive way of thinking. For example, in 1913 the explorer-anthropologist Vilhjalmur Stefansson described the traditional hunter-gatherer lifestyle of the far North in the following way:

> They gathered their food with the weapons of the men of the Stone Age, they thought their simple, primitive thoughts. . . . I had nothing to imagine; I had merely to look and listen; for here were not remains of the Stone Age, but the Stone Age itself.

Ironically, during this time, Stefansson, like other Europeans in the subarctic, had to depend on these "Stone Age" peoples in order to survive. Far from being ar-

An early-20th-century Chipewyan woman's dress, made of caribou hide and worn fur side out. The wrist cuffs of the dress are edged in dark striped cloth.

chaic or obsolete, the traditional skills and ways of life of the Chipewyans are still used today by those who wish to exploit the richness and bounty of Canada's subarctic.

But in one sense Stefansson was right—Chipewyan survival techniques do have a long and venerable history. Archaeologists studying prehistoric sites in North America have revealed that humans in the Canadian North have relied on the caribou for eons. Some 10,000 to 12,000 years ago, during the Great Ice Age, the ancestors of Native Americans entered Alaska either across a narrow stretch of ice covering what is now the Bering Strait or across a land bridge that once connected Siberia with Alaska. The people then moved south, eventually establishing populations throughout America. As the ice receded, corridors of land opened and small bands of nomadic hunters followed herds of migrating caribou northward, leaving traces of their lives in the form of small stone blades and tools of bone and wood as well as hearths containing the remains of caribou that they had killed and eaten. The caribou eventually reached the Arctic coast 1,000 years ago, the time at which the ancestors of the Chipewyans became established in the area of Canada that their descendants still occupy today—a territory larger than that of any other single Native American group in the entire continent of North America. The ancestors of the Chipewyans hunted caribou east of the Great Slave Lake, and each summer those living close to the tree line followed the migrating herds onto the Barren Grounds (the treeless plains of northern Canada located to the west of Hudson Bay) much like their descendants would.

In addition to material goods left in campsites, early Native Americans left

An engraving by fur trader Sir George Back captures the natural splendor of the Chipewyans' territory. Modern Chipewyans have aggressively lobbied the Canadian government to protect northern Canada's wilderness.

additional evidence of their migrations through their language. The Chipewyans form part of the Athapaskan language family, which contains tribes ranging from Alaska to Mexico. About 20 bands in Canada speak languages in the Athapaskan family; consequently, they are known as Northern Athapaskans. Of this group, the Chipewyans live the furthest east.

Today the Chipewyans live in one of the last great wild areas of North America. Their ancestral lands have clean air, pristine waterways, and an abundance of extraordinary animal and plant life. As with other native peoples of the north, respect and reciprocity for the land are a pillar of the Chipewyan way of life. That respect for the land has resulted in modern times in intense and successful lobbying by the Chipewyans and other Native Americans to have the Canadian government enact an aggressive environmental protection policy for northern Canada.

It is important to note that books such as this one that attempt to recount the history of the indigenous peoples of northern Canada tend to focus on the latter fraction of their 10,000-year history in North America. The Chipewyans and their neighbors did not originally have a written language, so there is a dearth of material concerning Chipewyan life before contact with the Europeans. Consequently, many history books give the impression that the culture and lives of tribes like the Chipewyans remained unchanged for the thousands of years before the first Europeans came to the area, an impression that is certainly inaccurate. In addition, most histories of the northern Canadian tribes split the events that occurred after the first contact with the Europeans into time divisions with names such as "Early Contact Period," "Stabilized Fur and Mission Period," and "Governmental-Industrial Period"—designations that see this history entirely in terms of a tribe's interactions with Europeans and Euro-Canadians.

Part of the reason for this bias is that the people who recorded these later events tended to be European or Euro-Canadian themselves. Consequently, they recorded selective aspects of Chipewyan culture, usually those aspects that were of direct economic or political interest or that they found especially curious or sensational. The result is an overlay of European and Euro-Canadian culture and its values upon the non-European culture of the Chipewyans, inevitably presenting a distorted picture of their culture and history—even the archaeological record left by Chipewyan ancestors is subject to interpretation in the context of a society with Western values and ideas. Searches for Chipewyan oral myths and traditions, and, more recently, recordings of their oral histories have been undertaken to try to bring in non-European points of view and restore some balance to the recorded history of northern Canada, as well as to gain a deeper understanding of traditional Chipewyan life in the Great White North.

A Barren Grounds caribou treks through a snow-covered field in this sketch. The caribou were a vital source of food and supplies to the Chipewyans.

STRATEGIES
FOR
SURVIVAL

According to David M. Smith in his book *Moose-Deer Island House People: A History of the Native People of Fort Resolution*: "It would be hard to overstress the importance of barren ground caribou for the aboriginal Chipewyan." Like the lakes and the rivers, the caribou were a feature of the northern Canadian landscape, a resource that Chipewyan myth linked forever to the land and the people. The two great movements of caribou—the migration south in the fall and the migration north in the spring—were not only essential hunting times (a good hunt could easily ensure meat for an entire season) but were also important social times that bound together the Chipewyan community. The Chipewyans spent much of the year traveling in separate small hunting bands consisting of one or a few nuclear families, but the caribou migration was a time for these families to gather together in large communal hunting groups that sometimes numbered up to 600 people.

One hunting strategy used at this time was the pound method, which required literally hundreds of men, women, and children to work together in a well-organized and coordinated group. The pound was a large (sometimes one mile in diameter), strong circular fence, made from brushy trees. The pound was always built in a wooded area at the very edge of the forest; inside the fence, mazelike counterhedges were arranged around the existing trees. In every opening the Chipewyan placed snares made of *babiche*, semi-tanned caribou or moose hide, which were firmly attached to logs or tree roots. The Chipewyans observed many rituals and taboos to ensure the pound's success, including avoiding walking in the pound and only touching the snares with mittens on their hands.

The pound was built on one of the caribou migration routes. Each caribou subherd often followed the same route for many years, although they could suddenly shift routes for no discernible reason. These paths were well studied by the Chipewyans (as were all caribou habits), who would make temporary settlements near the major ranges and paths of each subherd in order to more easily exploit the migrating animals. These settlements were usually on high ground to afford the Chipewyans a view of both the incoming caribou and the pound. When the herd was sighted, the Chipewyans moved into position for the kill.

While the pound itself was in the woods, its entrance was at the edge of the forest. Extending out from the entrance into the treeless area would be two long rows of stakes or brush with fluttering banners and moss on their tops, laid out in the shape of a funnel, with the wide opening at the entrance to the pound. The Chipewyans would chase the leaders of the approaching caribou herd into the funnel. Once the animals entered the funnel, the fluttering banners would scare them away from the stakes and toward the pound. When the caribou reached the pound, the women and children would take up posts outside the enclosure to prevent the escape of any loose animals. The men would enter the pound and kill the trapped caribou, stabbing the snared animals with stone or bone lances or daggers and shooting those not caught by the snares with stone or bone arrows.

Another form of communal hunt was the water drive, a technique used at river or lake crossings. The hunters would conceal themselves in canoes on both banks of the body of water that the caribou were to cross. Once the lead animals had gone halfway across the lake or river, the hunters on both banks would launch their canoes and lay them end to end, forming two booms in front of and behind the swimming animals. The end canoes would then swing about, enclosing the animals in a circle of canoes. This caused mass confusion and panic among the caribou as those in the lead attempted to retreat from the canoes in front while those in the rear pressed forward to escape the canoes behind them. The panicked creatures would begin to flounder, and the Chipewyan hunters in the canoes would move among the herd, killing the caribou with their lances. If the lead caribou actually succeeded in turning about and leading the herd in one direction again, the hunters would reposition their canoes in the boom formation and reencircle the herd, repeating the maneuver again and again until all the animals were killed.

The pound and water-drive strategies were lethal and efficient hunting techniques that ensured the deaths of virtually every caribou caught within their perimeters. Such carnage was deemed necessary, however, because the hunt had to supply each person in the large hunting group (along with any neighboring hunting group that had been less lucky hunting caribou) with meat, hides, and supplies for the next several months. Because everybody contributed to the hunt, everybody shared in the bounty of the kill. The sharing of food helped tie the disparate bands and families together into one hunting group, a tie strengthened by the elaborate group coordination required by these hunting techniques.

The times of plenty following the group hunts were occasions of great feasts for the Chipewyans. The women would start fires by using a fire-making fungus that grows on birch trees, rubbing it rapidly with a stone until it smoldered. Families would then cook the freshly killed caribou flesh on sticks over fires or would boil it in birch-bark containers sewn together with spruce roots and made watertight with spruce gum. These baskets were filled with water and meat, and then a shovel-rake fashioned from the antler of a caribou was used to trans-

fer hot stones from the fire to the containers. The hot rocks would boil the water, which would cook the meat.

Caribou tongue and, when in season, fetus, were and are considered delicacies by the Chipewyans. The udder of a milk-giving doe and the back fat were also choice morsels. Caribou blood was used to make soup, while caribou bones were cracked to extract their nutritious marrow and then boiled in kettles to render their valuable fat. The contents of a caribou's paunch, semi-digested lichens and other vegetation, were eaten raw or cooked or were made into a sort of Chipewyan steamed pudding. The pud-

A group of Chipewyans sit outside their caribou-hunting camp in this 1880 photograph. Both the tents in the background and the clothes on the people are made primarily of caribou skin.

ding was made by mixing the contents of a paunch with chopped meat, chewed fat, and water. This mixture was stuffed back into the stomach and hung in the heat and smoke of a fire for several days. When the stomach was distended by steam, the dish was ready to be enjoyed.

Caribou skin was of great value to the Chipewyans, but during the great spring migration the skin was of little use because great holes were made in it by gadflies, which deposit their eggs beneath the caribou skin. These eggs hatch in the spring, and the gadfly larvae eat their way through the skin of the caribou. The loss of the hides, however, was somewhat offset by the presence of the gadfly grubs, which were considered a delicacy and were harvested from the hides of killed caribou.

Of course, the important caribou hunts sometimes failed, a fact reflected in the Chipewyan saying, "No man knows the way of the wind and the caribou." If a fire blocked the caribou's pathway across the Barren Grounds, or if the caribou were offended by some lapse of ritual or a broken taboo, or if an evil Inuit sorcerer up north had successfully worked a malicious bit of magic, then the Chipewyans would wait in vain for the great herds.

Consequently, during times of plenty the Chipewyans always prepared for the uncertainties of the hunt and the constant cycle of feast and famine that is a harsh reality in the subarctic. Caribou meat was dried and smoked for future use and stored in bags made from strips of caribou leg hide. In order to make the dried meat more compact for travel, the women would jump on the prepared meat in its bags to pack it down more tightly. Women also prepared pemmican, a compact and highly nutritious food that keeps fairly well. To make pemmican, dried meat is pulverized with a hammer-stone and boiled with caribou fat. The resulting mixture is poured into caribou intestines and frozen in winter or cached up high in trees during the warmer months. Since these caches of pemmican were important survival staples, their sites of storage were marked with lobsticks, trees stripped of all their branches. (Disturbing another's cache was considered a gesture of extreme aggression.) Hunger was a threat all year round; while in warm months there was usually more game about, meat and pemmican reserves were more likely to spoil than in the cold.

Another hedge against starvation was rabbits snared by Chipewyan women. Rabbits, however, were a poor substitute for caribou, which can weigh up to 600 pounds apiece and have more calories per pound than rabbits due to their higher percentage of body fat. Beaver was also hunted in lean times, but while beavers are considerably fatter than rabbits, they were fairly rare in the traditional territory of the Chipewyans, and hunting them could be quite a time-consuming process. When all else failed, the Chipewyan women would scrape lichens off the rocks and boil these with water to make a thick gel; this gel was filling, if nutritionally poor, and was used to satisfy hungry children until game reappeared. Adults would chew the skins that their garments were made of to quiet their hunger pangs. Generally speaking, hunger was less of a threat if a band was mobile because the band could relocate to better hunting grounds or meet up with another band that would share its food; but hunger combined with any illness or lameness that adversely affected mobility was an immediate threat to survival.

Not only were caribou an essential source of food, but they were also used to make clothing and equipment. A woman preparing a caribou for the pot would carefully save the bladder for storing grease or oil, cut away the fibrous parts of the leg for sinew and thread, and put aside antler tines for the manufacture of cutting and scraping tools. Chipewyan women prepared caribou hides for use as clothing, tent, and sledge material by first stretching the skins to dry on frames of wood. Then they would make a mixture of caribou brains and melted snow and apply it to the stretched skins to begin the tanning process. After the mixture had dried, the skin was scraped to remove the hair, and finally it was cured in the smoke of a fire. Babiche, used for snares, bows, fishing nets, and snowshoe webbing, was also made from caribou skins. To make babiche the skins were dried and scraped of hair, but instead of being cured they were laid flat on the ground and a spiral cut was made counterclockwise from the outer edge of the skin to its center, resulting in a long, thin strip of leather.

After the fall migration the caribou would disperse into their wintering ground. The Chipewyans would dis-perse as well, breaking into small hunting bands and adopting different strategies for exploiting the caribou. These strategies reflected the Chipewyan hunters' intimate knowledge of caribou habits. For example, in October, during the rutting season, the Chipewyans used special lures made of a few pieces of caribou antler tied in a bunch and attached to a hunter's belt. When the hunter moved, the antlers would rattle against one another, producing a sound that resembles that made by two male caribou fighting for the favor of a cow. When two males are busy fighting, there is often an opportunity for a third caribou male to mate clandestinely with the cow, and the Chipewyan lure was quite effective at attracting caribou bulls.

Another method, employed by pairs of hunters, was to walk in such a way that one hunter was hidden behind his partner, making them appear to be a single person. The hunters would walk toward and then away from a caribou, arousing the animal's curiosity. The caribou would cautiously follow the hunter, taking care to keep out of bow range, and one of the hunters would duck out of sight behind a rock or clump of spruce as his partner continued walking. When the caribou passed the hidden hunter, the hunter would ambush him with a bow or spear.

When the ground was covered with deep snow, the Chipewyan hunter would strap on snowshoes made of birchwood and babiche and track single caribou. Although the caribou has a wide hoof, it still sinks into the snow, while a hunter

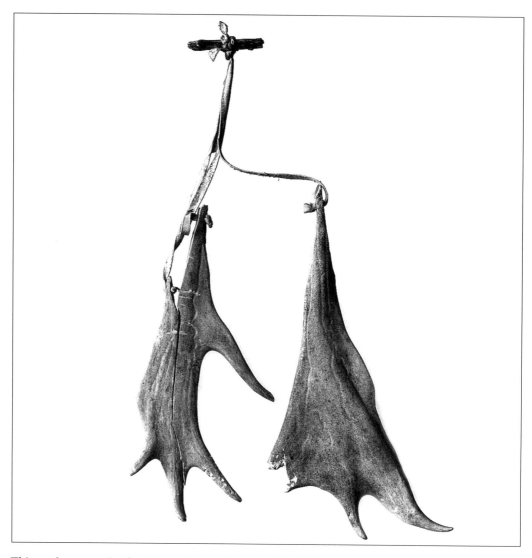

This rattle was made of caribou antlers and was used by Chipewyan hunters to attract male caribou.

wearing snowshoes can travel with relative ease and speed over the surface of the snow. A Chipewyan hunter with snowshoes could track a lone caribou and run it to exhaustion, making for an easy kill. (This technique also worked well with moose.) If the animal was too heavy or too far from the hunter's camp to carry back, it was immediately skinned and its meat was buried in the snow. The cache would be marked with lobsticks so that the hunter or another member of his band could easily find and retrieve the meat at a later time.

Another hunting tool used by the Chipewyans to exploit the caribou and other animals was that of *inkonze,* or magical knowledge. Inkonze, which literally means "to know a little something," was a valuable asset for the Chipewyan hunter. Inkonze was based on the Chipewyan belief that spirits reside in all aspects of the natural environment—rivers, rocks, trees, wind, snow, humans, and caribou—and influence every aspect of life.

Perhaps the most important of the spirits as far as survival was concerned were animal spirits. If offended, animal spirits would make sure that the hunts failed, so respect—in the form of following taboos—had to be shown them at all times. The Chipewyans saw a successful hunt as an agreement between equal partners: the animals agreed to be hunted, and the hunters agreed to treat the animals with respect by observing certain rituals and taboos. For example, the tongue and fat of the first animal of the season caught in a snare were hung up on a tree as a gesture of respect and thanks to the spirits. Some practices were a little more manipulative; whenever a caribou was killed, the Chipewyans were sure to cut off its muzzle, where the soul of the caribou was believed to reside, to prevent the animal from telling other caribou of its fate.

Observing taboos helped to keep a person's inkonze strong. Omens, charms, and amulets also formed a part of a person's inkonze; for example, a hunter might possess a magical song giving him access to the power of certain animals. But inkonze was inherent within a person, and a song that increased one hunter's inkonze was useless to the next, who had a different sort of inkonze or perhaps lacked it altogether. A person knew that he had inkonze by his dreams. Repeated dreams about a certain animal were especially significant, for they meant that the spirit of that animal had taken an interest in a person and might teach him how to tap that power in later dreams.

Knowing more about one's inkonze was important because it came in different types, and proficiency in one sort of inkonze did not necessarily translate into proficiency with the others. One type of inkonze allowed hunters to make contact with their prey in dreams before the hunt. The spirit of a particular caribou would meet the spirit of a hunter in the hunter's dream. Then, when the hunter set off to search for the caribou, he would find the same animal he had met in his dream. The caribou, recognizing the hunter from the dream, would allow itself to be killed.

Another type of inkonze allowed the adept to determine what the future held for him and his followers. This inkonze could be used to determine where to find game and what the weather would be like—valuable assets for a group whose survival depended upon hunting. It could also be used to foretell attacks from hostile groups of Crees or Inuits, the traditional enemies of the Chipewyans, and could save the group from the disaster of an assault.

The third type of inkonze, and the only type that could be practiced by women, was curing inkonze, used to heal the sick. Practitioners of curing inkonze could put themselves into a trance and converse with the spirit world. With the help of a guardian spirit, the practitioner would ascertain which evil spirits had caused the illness, then drive them off through a display of power. Sickness-bearing spirits could also be extracted from the body of the ill person by sucking

or blowing through a special bone tube. Drums and rattles were sometimes used to contact animal spirits and request their aid or to drive away the malicious spirits who had caused the sickness.

A person who could marshal the arts of inkonze could readily claim a position of leadership within a band. People were not supposed to discuss their inkonze, so band members had to look for signs of skill with inkonze. One such sign was repeated success in hunting—a man who had powerful inkonze usually had plenty of food and could support many wives. Other members of the community

A group of hunters on snowshoes stand proudly by their caribou prey in this photograph, taken in 1908 or 1909. Among the Chipewyans, hunting was necessary for survival and also integrally associated with spirituality and masculinity.

would also pay a man (not with money, which was a foreign concept to the Chipewyans, but with services) to use his inkonze to divine the future, cure the sick, or give advice, further increasing both his wealth and status.

Although it was believed that children of people with strong inkonze were more likely to have strong inkonze themselves, there was no guarantee that this would happen, and each individual had to demonstrate the strength of his own inkonze if he wished to have influence within the community. The same was true for all leadership abilities, for there was no chiefly or royal class among the Chipewyans. Leadership of a group was usually assumed by the group member with the most important skill for the survival of the entire band—namely, the ability to successfully hunt caribou—and leadership was relatively informal, with a leader being viewed as the first among equals rather than as a superior being. With the exception of the biannual communal hunts and the occasional summer festivities, the Chipewyans lived in small, family-based hunting bands; consequently, rigid and complex hierarchical social structures were unnecessary. If a man wanted to influence a larger number of bands and could support many wives, he would take wives from different bands, thus giving him family ties and a certain amount of status in each band,

and an especially ambitious older man could sometimes get several young warriors to follow him and intimidate other bands into accepting his influence. But for the most part, leaders were simply the most experienced and best hunters in a group, and their power was limited to deciding where and what to hunt.

In any case, if old age or infirmity hindered a leader's hunting success, his group would quickly change its allegiance and follow someone who could better help them survive in the harsh subarctic environment. Even such shifts in leadership could be quite informal, especially in very small bands where the members were all part of one nuclear family. Oftentimes the father would be considered in charge until well past his prime, even if most of the actual decision-making responsibilities had already devolved to one of his sons.

The social institutions of the Chipewyans formed a part of the survival strategies that helped them successfully exploit the resources in their environment. But human life is more than group survival. A culture or way of life helps define each group of people, giving each person a specific identity within the larger mass of humanity. The Chipewyan way of life marked them as a distinct tribe, giving them cultural cohesion and allowing them to endure as a people for generation after generation.

A Chipewyan woman pounds dried meat into powder to make pemmican.

THE
CHIPEWYAN
CYCLE
OF
LIFE

When [the wind] blows stronger, when the snow melts, when the caribou lose the hair from their antlers, when the frost arrives, when the caribou antlers are shed, when the caribou are with calf— these were some of the months of the Chipewyan year. Birth, death, and regeneration defined the seasons of the Chipewyan year as well as the seasons of human life, and both sorts of seasons were marked by preparations, celebrations, precautions, rituals, and traditions.

Every Chipewyan wore a special amulet around his neck that contained a piece of his umbilical cord sewn into a small pouch, worn from the day of birth until the day of death. The amulet was believed to protect the wearer from harm as he passed through life. To ensure that her baby would be healthy and strong, a Chipewyan woman observed many taboos during her pregnancy, including avoiding eating caribou fetus or sitting on a sledge. When the time of birth ar-

rived and the group was in a camp, a special tent or brush structure would be built for the woman, or if birth was imminent her family would simply abandon their tent for her use. A number of women would attend the birth, sometimes aiding the birth process by pulling a wide belt of caribou skin across the mother's abdomen to help the infant descend. Like many hunting societies, the Chipewyan believed that blood from women was offensive to animal spirits and would bring bad luck to any man or any hunting weapon that came into contact with it, so when a birth was about to occur the men were sure to remove all weapons from the vicinity and absent themselves from the site. A woman who had given birth was considered hazardous to men for a month after the childbirth, and during this period she was attended solely by women. The child was under a similar taboo, and the father was not allowed to see his child until a month had passed.

33

Despite this reverence given the birth process, the Chipewyan migratory way of life sometimes did not allow the group to stop and camp for prolonged periods. A band in need of food had no choice but to pursue a likely quarry, no matter what. Under these circumstances, a pregnant Chipewyan woman would travel with the group as long as she could, then go off with a few attendants when birth was imminent. If labor was in short supply, the woman might have to give birth alone, then pick up her belongings and rejoin the band, keeping her distance so as not to pollute the men. This was undoubtedly a severe hardship, but group survival was always the paramount consideration.

The child-rearing duties of Chipewyan women were made more complicated because women were also responsible for transporting equipment from camp to camp. Chipewyan men needed mobility during journeys so that they could pursue game or defend the group from enemy attack; consequently, Chipewyan women had to carry camp equipment and pull heavy sledges packed with tents and necessities. Although the Chipewyans attempted to take as little as possible with them from camp to camp, the women were often so heavily burdened that they rested by leaning against a tree or rock for fear they could not get up again if they lay on the ground. In order to take care of infants and keep them warm while carrying these burdensome loads, Chipewyan mothers would carry their babies under their clothing and next to their skin. The infant was held in place by a belt which passed from the middle of the mother's back over her shoulders and breasts, and moss was used as a diaper to keep the babies dry. These techniques left the mother's hands free for carrying and pulling camp equipment.

In later years the Chipewyans used dogs to pull the sledges, a technique which they learned from neighboring tribes. They also adopted the custom from their Cree neighbors of using infant carrying bags, which were made of caribou hides and lined with hareskin in the winter. Moss was packed in the bags as a sort of diaper for the baby. As the Chipewyans made more contact with other indigenous peoples in northern Canada, they adopted another infant-carrying device called the carrying cradle. This device used a backboard with a carrying strap to which a caribou-skin carrying bag was attached. The bag laced up the front with a piece of babiche to keep the infant securely in place. As infants grew older they were carried by means of a baby belt, which passed around the child's bottom and over the mother's shoulders. Both of these apparatuses were usually elaborately embroidered by affectionate Chipewyan mothers.

The Chipewyan often named male children for an event at the time of their birth, a dream, or something distinctive about the child itself. Girls' names frequently included the word for the small, fur-bearing marten, *tha.* Typical names (translated into English) might be Marten's Heart, White Marten, or Summer

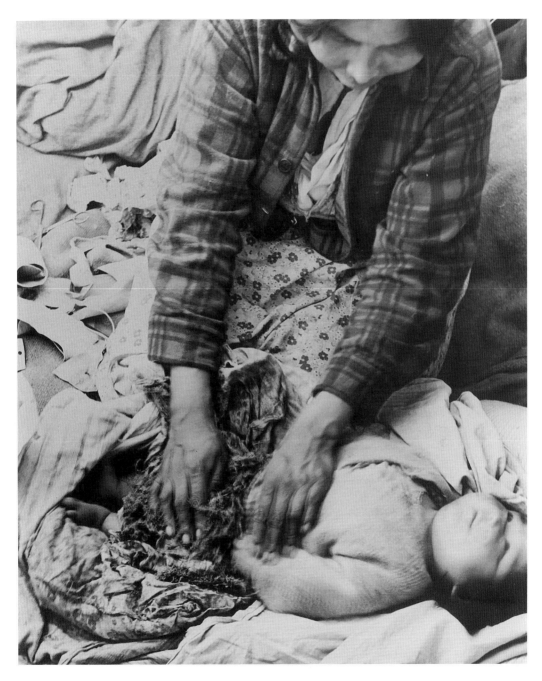

A woman packs an infant-carrying bag with absorbent dried moss. The Chipewyans readily adopted useful child-carrying technologies from other tribes.

Marten. The migratory way of life of the Chipewyans meant that all members of the group had to contribute, and boys and girls were no exception. Children gathered firewood and water, tended snares, and stoned birds. There was early and significant segregation between the genders among the Chipewyans. Boys learned hunting, trapping, and fishing skills from the older males in the group. These were skills upon which the group's survival would ultimately depend, and boys were strongly encouraged to develop them. Boys would start hunting seriously at age 14 or 15 (although it usually took another decade for them to become truly adept hunters), and the first large game animal killed by a boy was an occasion for celebration.

Because hunting was so closely associated with inkonze, Chipewyan boys learned about more than the terrain, the habits of animals, and the numerous hunting strategies. They were also instructed in the making of amulets and talismans, as well as the carrying out of rituals and the correct observance of taboos. A Chipewyan boy learned that if he wanted to be a swift runner, he had to drink water made only from the soft snow under the heavier top crust because water made from the heavy top snow would make one slow, no matter how fast one tried to run. So too, a hunter had to avoid eating bear paws if he wanted to remain light on his feet. Boys were carefully instructed to hang the first kill of the day from a tree branch as an offering to the animal spirits in acknowledgment of their help.

The Chipewyan boys also learned the proper rituals for fishing. The bills and feet of gulls, loons, or geese were attached to the head- and foot-ropes of the net. The toes and jaws of otters—proficient animal fishers—were fastened at the four corners of the net. When the first fish was caught, it was broiled whole in a fire as a first-catch ritual. The flesh was carefully stripped off without breaking a single bone, and the entire fish skeleton was then burnt in the flames.

The fishing nets themselves were believed to have spirits, and boys learned the proper way to show them respect. When Chipewyans fished in rivers or narrow channels that joined two lakes, they scattered their nets at great distances from one another instead of tying several nets together; if the nets were kept close it was believed that each net would become jealous of its neighbor. If this happened, the nets would not catch a single fish.

The maintenance of the camp was the sphere of Chipewyan women—and more often than not their work was exacting, arduous, and never-ending. Caribou skins wore out fairly quickly, so each article of clothing, each babiche implement, and each lodge covering had to be made from new skins every year. The average member of a Chipewyan band needed to have 20 caribou skins prepared, cut, and sewn into clothing each year; additional skins had to be prepared to make tents and sleeping bags. Chipewyan girls were quickly put to work helping to prepare skins and to manufacture clothing and shelter.

A Chipewyan Métis (mixed Chipewyan and European) woman, Catherine Beaulieu Lafferty, poses with her two sons, James (left) and Edward, in this 1914 photograph. Chipewyan boys began honing their hunting skills at an early age.

Chipewyan boys and girls did enjoy a variety of amusements and sports, however. Entertainment equipment was, like so many other things, made from caribou. Caribou-skin balls stuffed with moss were used in a kind of stickball game. Chipewyan girls played a ring-and-pin game with six pierced caribou toe-joints threaded onto a long piece of babiche, which was attached to a stick at the other end. The object of the game was to toss the bones in the air and catch them on the stick. Another children's toy was the bull-roarer, a toy made of a thin slab of notched wood attached to a long babiche cord. When the toy was whirled in the air it emitted a low noise like the roaring of a bull. A spinning toy was made from a thong of babiche threaded with a caribou vertebra in the center. When the thong was twirled the vertebra would move back and forth along it as the player manipulated the thong. A pea-shooter was made from a hollow swan wingbone; Chipewyan children shot spitballs made of chewed lichen through the bone. Fathers also made smaller versions of bows and arrows for their sons, and mothers made dolls with carrying cradles for their daughters.

The most popular Chipewyan entertainment was storytelling, which was enjoyed by the young and the old alike. Each evening, tales were told about past feats of heroism, about the beginning of the world, and about the different animals in the tundra, the taiga, and the woods—especially the caribou. While the stories were told, the men would smoke willow-wood pipes filled with a type of fungus that grows on birch trees, while the women engaged in quiet work such as twisting willow-bark fiber into twine for fishing nets, decorating baby belts with colored porcupine quills (or, in later times, with European glass beads), and making yarn from the fur of rabbits they had snared earlier.

Chipewyan tales often featured characters called culture heroes, who embodied and reinforced the values of the society. Young, strong, and admirable characters, Chipewyan culture heroes exhibited the self-reliance and survival skills necessary to ensure their band's survival. Reciting these stories and myths was an essential means of maintaining and transmitting the traditions of the Chipewyan way of life. Stories were also told about various types of humans and near-humans, later called bushmen or bogeymen by English-speakers, who lurked in the bush, stole goods, attacked women, and kidnapped children.

While culture heroes were considered figures from the past, bushmen for the most part were (and are) considered a real day-to-day threat by the Chipewyans. There is no one word for such people in Chipewyan; instead several names exist to describe different sorts of bushmen, including the *udzena dene,* insane or criminal people; the *ene dene,* "enemy people" (formerly members of the hostile Cree and Inuit tribes); and the *amoo,* simple monsters. Bushmen are still an accepted part of Chipewyan culture; according to anthropologist Henry S. Sharp in his *The Transformation of Bigfoot:*

Maleness, Power, and Belief Among the Chipewyan:

> In the summer of 1984, [a Chipewyan town] was troubled by a series of bogeymen. Several men, apparently survivalists or members of a paramilitary organization, spent two weeks living in the bush in the vicinity of the village. They wore black fabric jumpsuitlike garments, likened by the local Chipewyan to skindiver's wet suits, complete with military webbing and attached pouches, survival gear (including large switch-blade knives) and token camouflage. They were not very adept at avoiding contact and were seen many times by residents . . . along the roads near the village and in the surrounding bush. These people engaged in no hostile activity but they refused to answer when they were spoken to. The Chipewyan always addressed them and offered assistance when they were seen, but the men always silently withdrew into the bush. Before the two weeks were up, they had so thoroughly established themselves as bogeymen that several times Chipewyan men fired upon them when they did not respond to being hailed.

Generally only young children were and are afraid of the amoo, which supposedly skulk around at night making strange noises and looking for disobedient and tender young Chipewyans to steal, but as the above account demonstrates, reasonable adults were and are concerned about the udzena and ene dene, often with good reason. As Sharp points out, "A major reason the Chipewyan have a bogeyman figure is because there are bogeymen."

While for Chipewyan boys the privileges and responsibilities of adulthood were granted gradually as they became better hunters, for girls adulthood was definitely reached upon menarche. The taboos regarding women's blood forced the adolescent girl to be separated from the group during her menstruation; in addition, she had to wear a garment that completely hid her face. She had to observe many other taboos as well, including not touching the men's hunting implements and not walking over a man's tracks. Failure to observe these taboos, it was believed, would bring disaster upon the group: the animals would be offended by the blood, the hunts would fail, and the girl herself would get sick and perhaps die.

Once menstruation began, a girl was considered to be of marriageable age. Since a man had to be a good provider to be considered eligible for marriage, and generally a man was in his mid-twenties before he was truly skilled at hunting, Chipewyan girls of 12 or 13 were quite often married to men twice their age. Some girls were betrothed when they were children, and there was no formal ceremony to mark the event of marriage; a newly married couple began their life together by residing with the parents of the bride, usually until their first child was born, at which time the couple moved into a separate household. This living arrangement worked out to be a sort of bride price, since any game that the husband killed while living with the bride's parents would be shared among all members of her family. In addition, once a couple married, their families shared a special bond. Siblings-in-law (especially brothers-in-law) were supposed to work closely together and support one another completely, and not only did the parents of the married couple also consider each other siblings-in-law, but they often arranged the marriage precisely to obtain this sort of relationship with each other. Divorce (which often marked the breakdown of the family alliance as well as the marriage itself) was somewhat casual, although usually complicated by the emotional issues that had broken up the marriage and by the dependence of Chipewyan women on men as providers. A husband could simply leave his wife, but if a wife left her husband she had to be sure she had a man to move in with (usually either her

This 1948 photograph shows two Chipewyan girls softening a caribou skin by pulling on it. Adult women expected girls to help them in the arduous tasks of preparing and preserving caribou and other prey.

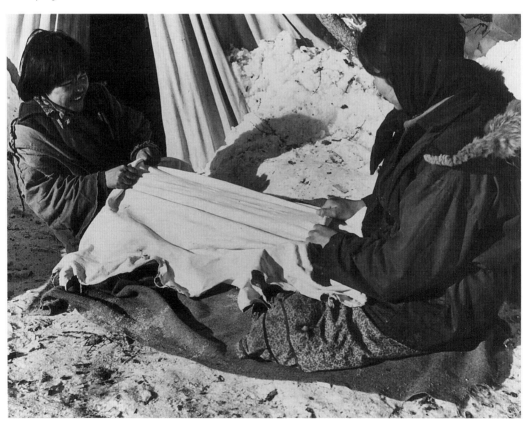

new husband or a family member); otherwise she would have no food and was more vulnerable to attack by her sometimes violently disgruntled ex-husband. A marriage could also be ended if a husband lost his wife while wife wrestling. Wife wrestling—really more of a hair- and ear-pulling contest that tested a man's ability to withstand pain rather than his balance or physical strength— occurred when one man decided he desired the wife of another and challenged him to a match. If a man lost his wife in such a contest he also lost a good deal of status and generally was too humiliated and embarrassed by the event to ever try to win her back.

In addition to providing meat, the Chipewyan husband was responsible for defending his family against enemy attacks. The traditional enemies of the Chipewyans were the Crees to the south and the Inuits to the north, and all three groups launched constant attacks and counterattacks against each other in retaliation for supposed incidents of trespass or sorcery or in revenge for earlier attacks. The Chipewyan warrior used the same weapons to kill man as he used to kill caribou, arming himself with lances, daggers, and bows and arrows. For protection he depended upon a wooden shield and help from the spirits. Each man painted his shield with magical signs and symbols designed to help him kill enemies and protect him from being killed. Raids in the subarctic were serious business; generally speaking, during a raid all the men of the enemy camp were killed, and the women and children were only spared for purposes of enslavement.

Warfare, hunting, and constant traveling required a great deal of physical hardiness from each individual Chipewyan. Consequently, old age was hardly an easy time. The diminished skill in hunting and lessened mobility that are often a part of aging could strain the resources of the group to which the elderly person belonged and endanger its survival, especially during lean times or when the person was extremely decrepit or ill. Consequently, elderly or ill people who could not keep up with the group were sometimes abandoned. Such abandonment was considered acceptable because the person was sure to die anyway; it was considered better to leave an individual to perish than to endanger the whole group with the prospect of starvation. Although such behavior might seem callous, the Chipewyans were by no means insensible to the tragedy involved, and people were only abandoned when there was simply no other option. The surviving band members provided some food and a shelter for the person abandoned and mourned their lost relative intensely, wailing and crying for the deceased, destroying their tent and goods, and strictly avoiding the place where the person had died or been abandoned.

No matter what the circumstances of a death, burial was impractical in the frozen ground of northern Canada, so Chipewyan bodies were wrapped in hide and left in the open. There they were often devoured by beasts and birds of prey; as a result, the Chipewyans would

A large Chipewyan family poses with their dogs for this 1894 photograph, taken in Manitoba, Canada. The Chipewyans have strong and complex family ties that are reflected in a dizzying array of kin terms, which have yet to be fully catalogued.

not eat the flesh of foxes, ravens, or wolves. It was believed that if the appropriate taboos were followed, the person's soul would travel through the earth by stone canoe, eventually crossing a lake to a place where life began again.

When groups that had been apart for a season met again, they first greeted each other by an elaborate recitation of the season's misfortunes. Seated in two groups about 20 yards from one another, one elder person from each family listed the deaths and tragedies that had be-fallen his group, while the women of the group wailed at each mention of death or misfortune. Only when the recitation had ended would the two groups meet each other with an exchange of happier news and gifts.

These were the aspects of life that defined the Chipewyans as a people and gave them an identity that enabled them to transcend time with their sense as a people intact. The preparations, celebra-tions, precautions, rituals, and traditions of the Chipewyans evolved and changed over many millennia. The cultural flexi-bility of the Chipewyans let them make adjustments to changes in season, in the environment, and at each phase of life. But this same flexibility made them highly susceptible to external pressures, and the coming of the Europeans to the North American continent would create a variety of strong pressures on the Chipewyan people.

A rather fanciful European engraving shows a group of beavers happily at work. Beaver hunters would be the first Europeans to settle in northern Canada.

THE
ARRIVAL
OF
THE
EUROPEANS

The European invasion and settlement of the Americas began in the 15th century as a different type of enterprise—namely, a search for a trade route to Asia that would avoid the existing long and treacherous route overland through territories controlled by hostile Muslim powers. Indeed, when the 15th-century explorer Christopher Columbus landed in America, he was so convinced that he had reached the Indies—a rather vague 15th-century geographical entity that included China, Japan, and India—that he named the land's inhabitants Indians, a misnomer that has survived to this day. Although Columbus died believing that he had reached the Indies, other Europeans soon realized that he had landed on a completely different continent, one that inconveniently blocked a direct water route from Europe to Asia. Attempts were promptly made to discover a means of sailing around this continent. A southern passage was eventually found, but

going around the southern end of the continent was a long and difficult journey, and the search continued for what was called the Northwest Passage, a feasible trade route around the northern end of the American continent. The quest for this passage eventually brought the Europeans to the Great White North, where the sea ice and frigid climate stymied their attempts to find the passage. There, they met Canada's indigenous population and encountered *Castor canadensis*, the North American beaver.

In 1610, Henry Hudson, an English explorer aboard the ship *Discovery*, sailed through a strait into the great inland sea of northern Canada that would later be known as Hudson Bay. During this voyage Hudson traded a knife, a looking glass, and some buttons for two beaver pelts from a lone Cree hunter. Although Hudson failed in his quest to discover the Northwest Passage and ultimately lost his life on this journey, he did find a new source of riches for the Europeans—the beaver pelts found in the interior of the Great White North.

During the 17th century beaver pelts from North America became prized items in Europe, and by the 18th century beaver had become the world's most valuable fur. Beaver fur was pressed into a thick felt, which was used to make elegant beaver hats that were both a fashionable way to keep dry (this was before the invention of the umbrella) and a highly visible indicator of social status. Beaver hats were so durable—and so expensive—that a man might buy just one small hat to last a lifetime, and a luxuriously large or high beaver hat indicated to all in view that its wearer was a person of wealth and status. The popularity and value of beaver piqued the interest of a number of British businessmen, and in 1668 two disenchanted French-Canadian explorers and fur traders, Pierre Esprit Radisson and Médard Chouart des Groseilliers (known to generations of Canadian schoolchildren as "Radishes and Gooseberries"), convinced a group of British investors that easy access to the best fur land lay to the north through Hudson Bay. In 1670, King Charles II of England granted a royal charter to establish the Hudson's Bay Company to exploit *Castor canadensis* and send its precious furs from Canada back to Europe.

The Hudson's Bay Company's charter included a land grant—the most generous land grant ever given a subject by a monarch. The limits of the company's territory were set at the head of all rivers or streams that drained into Hudson Bay—a huge area comprising roughly 40 percent of modern Canada plus the American states of Minnesota and North Dakota, and including the traditional territory of the Chipewyans. During the first 10 years of its existence the Hudson's Bay Company established a series of "factories" (so named after the "factors," the men in charge of company business and accounts, who lived there) along the coast of the bay. Two hundred men, recruited from the British Isles, were posted at these factories in order to exploit the company's immense territorial grant.

This small number of men was not nearly enough to effectively exploit the resources of such a huge area directly, nor could the men even ensure their own survival. The soil in the area surrounding Hudson Bay is too poor to grow the crops that make up a large part of the European diet, and the winters are too severe to raise cattle or sheep for meat. Europeans generally live in settled villages; consequently, the men of the Hudson's Bay Company were not willing to follow migratory animals such as the caribou, thus losing a potential steady source of food. Annual ships sent from England provided the men with some supplies, but the cost of transporting huge amounts of food across the Atlantic was prohibitive. Not surprisingly, the factory men soon began to depend on the surrounding tribes for their survival, first hiring bands of Crees and, later, bands of Chipewyans to act as "home guards," providing the factories with game. Since the Native

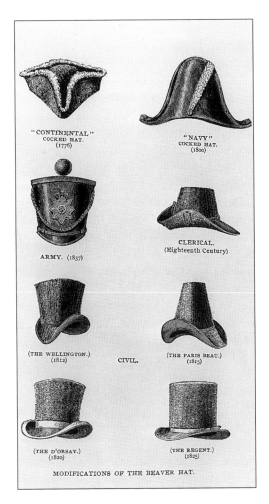

"CONTINENTAL" COCKED HAT. (1776).

"NAVY" COCKED HAT. (1800).

ARMY. (1837).

CLERICAL. (Eighteenth Century).

(THE WELLINGTON.) (1812).

CIVIL.

(THE PARIS BEAU.) (1815).

(THE D'ORSAY.) (1820).

(THE REGENT.) (1825).

MODIFICATIONS OF THE BEAVER HAT.

An 1892 engraving illustrates different styles (both military and civil) of men's beaver hats that were popular in the late 18th and early 19th centuries.

Americans of the region knew the land and the habits of its animals better than the Europeans, they were much better fur trappers. Consequently, the Europeans also depended upon the indigenous peoples for the success of their business ven-

ture—a dependence that would continue for the next 300 years.

Naturally, the Native Americans of the area were not going to work for the Europeans without getting something in return, and the annual supply ship outfitted each factory with numerous goods, including metal implements, woven cloth, and guns and ammunition imported specifically for trade with the native customers. All the Hudson's Bay Company's factories were initially situated in Cree territory, and long before the Chipewyans ever saw the Europeans, they saw their commodities through trade with the Crees. The Chipewyans discovered that European iron chisels made fishing holes in frozen lakes more quickly and easily than traditional bone or stone tools. European metal knives quickly became widely used among the Chipewyans to skin and butcher caribou, and metal axes were used to more efficiently gather firewood.

The Chipewyans also discovered that European guns in Cree hands vastly deteriorated their own security. The Hudson's Bay Company traders readily traded flintlock muskets to the Crees because guns made them more efficient hunters who could provide more animal pelts for trade. Of course, firearms also dramatically improved the Crees' fighting capabilities, making them a far more deadly enemy to the Chipewyans or any other hostile tribe. Since the Hudson's Bay Company factories were located in Cree territory, the Crees could fairly easily prevent other tribes from trading directly with the Europeans, and Cree traders would simply refuse to trade guns, giving the tribe sole access to these powerful weapons.

But the Crees were ultimately stymied in their efforts to keep firearms from other tribes by the European traders themselves. Their control over the fur trade increased costs for the Hudson's Bay Company, which quickly became eager to trade directly with other tribes. Company traders first learned of the Chipewyans from Chipewyan women and children who had been taken captive by the Crees during raids, and on May 21, 1680, a company communiqué called for the establishment of Fort Prince of Wales where the New Severn (now Churchill) River flowed into Hudson Bay. The factory was deliberately built to the north of Cree territory in order to facilitate trade with the more northern tribes, especially the Chipewyans.

Trade—and access to firearms—immediately and profoundly affected the Chipewyans' lives. Beavers are scarce in the Chipewyan's traditional territory because they prefer the woodlands to the south of the best caribou-hunting areas, where the trees they use to build their dams are abundant. As a result, a number of Chipewyan bands moved permanently to the southern boreal forests to the north and south of Lake Athabasca, taking over territory that had traditionally been that of the Cree, adopting many Algonquin survival strategies, and eventually more than doubling Chipewyan territory. Increased competition for beaver and territory meant increased intertribal warfare; increased warfare meant an increased need for European guns and ammunition.

In addition, the food animals in the southern woodlands were quite different from those further north. The Chipewyans were so efficient in hunting caribou using their traditional methods that guns were unnecessary, but such hunting strategies were far less effective on the woodlands bison and moose, and guns became essential survival tools for the more southern bands. The Europeans were also willing to trade foodstuffs for fur—indeed, they encouraged such trade in the hope that the Native Americans would stop subsistence hunting altogether and focus all their energies on obtaining furs—and many southern Chipewyans began to rely on European foodstuffs for a significant portion of their diet.

Chipewyan society was also changed by the demands of the fur trade. Because hunting and trapping beaver did not require the large-scale cooperation that hunting caribou did, the exploitation of fur-bearing animals put an individual's hunting ability ahead of the communal cooperation that had characterized the Chipewyan way of life for generations. This shift from communal hunting and sharing to individual hunting resulted in the establishment and acceptance of concepts of individual ownership of traplines and hunting territories that had been previously considered community property. Chipewyan society was further splintered because of the distance the Chipewyans needed to travel to reach the factories along the shore of Hudson Bay.

(Continued on page 57)

THE
LAND
OF
LITTLE
FLOWERS

Although life was often strenuous for Chipewyan women, there were periods of rest. The long, subarctic winters of northern Canada limited outdoor activity for everyone; in addition, women were isolated and restricted to special tents during menstruation. Chipewyan women used these times of restricted activity to create elaborately ornamented clothing, decorating hide outfits with dyed moose hair or dyed porcupine or goose quills woven into decorative strips or sewn onto the hide with sinew.

The arrival of the Grey Nuns in Chipewyan territory in 1857 had a tremendous impact on Chipewyan handicrafts. European-style embroidery was taught and encouraged at the mission schools run by the nuns; Chipewyan women, in turn, already valued fine handiwork and ornate clothing and were eager to learn this new skill. The elaborate floral patterns popular among 19th-century Europeans soon caught on in "the land of little sticks" and replaced the earlier geometric designs. In addition, the stiff quills were eventually supplanted by materials that were easier to work into floral designs, such as small glass and metal beads, silk embroidery floss, cotton thread, wool yarn, and dyed horsehair. Some of the floral designs on these pages were inspired by flowers indigenous to northern Canada or by pictures of exotic flowers found in books or magazines. But most are traditional, stylized designs that are the truly original creations of Chipewyan women.

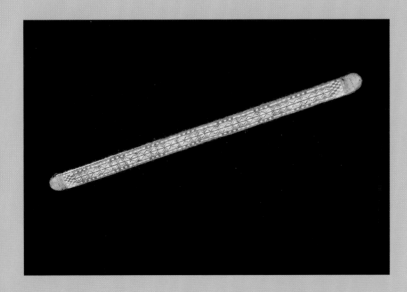

A Chipewyan baby belt, decorated with a traditional geometric design made from woven sinew and colored quills. The edges have been decorated with metal beads.

A 19th-century beaded sled dog blanket from the Great Slave Lake–Mackenzie River region of Canada. On festive occasions, sled dog teams were dressed up by attaching such fancy blankets to the dogs' ordinary harnesses with leather thongs. This blanket has a tall tasseled horn (a design element that also improved visibility in bad weather) and bells.

A beaded "octopus bag," so named for its unique shape. The origin of the octopus bag is not clear; it may have evolved from a fringed rectangular design or may have been adopted by the Chipewyans from the Crees.

51

These mittens, made around 1860 by a Chipewyan-Cree Métis artist, are made from caribou hide and decorated with white velvet embroidered with silk floss. The colorful cuffs and fringe are made from silk ribbon.

The cuffs of these fringed mittens are made of beaded black cloth, but the designs on the hand have been beaded directly onto the leather. The centers of the flowers and the leaves are made of metal beads.

A pair of beaded and fur-edged moccasins made by contemporary Chipewyan-Cree Métis artist Maria Houle.

The seamed and pointed toes of these moccasins are an older style that was gradually replaced with a seamless, rounded toe during the 20th century. When worn, the flaps around the ankles are turned up and secured with the attached cords, making a sort of low boot.

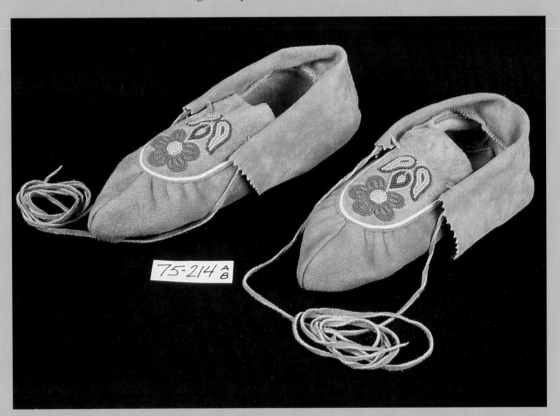

A pair of high boots, decorated with fur, leather fringe, and beading. The toes of these moccasins are the more modern rounded type.

(Continued from page 48)

Trading trips took hunters away from family members who depended upon them for a steady supply of meat and for defense against enemies.

The loose political structure of Chipewyan society was somewhat altered as well. European traders appointed certain hunters as trading chiefs of their bands, giving them special regalia, including uniforms, medals, and sashes. This new kind of leader played a role almost identical to that of the traditional hunting leader within a band, but with two important differences. In addition to his other duties, the trading chief was expected to negotiate issues with the Europeans, and consequently he had to be an articulate and charismatic man who would be a talented advocate for his band in addition to being an experienced hunter. Another difference was that a band's choice of trading chief had to be approved by and receive his regalia from the European traders before his position was considered official by either the Europeans or the

This 1743 watercolor-and-ink drawing delineates the various stages of the beaver hunt. Traditionally, the Chipewyans rarely hunted beaver, but shortly after the Hudson's Bay Company established its factories in Canada, many bands began to concentrate on fur gathering.

A Native American man exchanges fur for a flintlock rifle in this depiction of an 18th-century trading post. Guns were a common trade item and were used by the Chipewyans for both hunting and defense.

Chipewyans. This was a telling shift in power, indicating at least on a symbolic level a considerable loss in Chipewyan self-sufficiency and autonomy.

These adaptations went through many stages as contact with Europeans increased over time and different bands of Chipewyans participated in the fur trade to different extents. Some bands remained in the north, pursuing a traditional lifestyle, rarely utilizing firearms, and only trading with the Europeans caribou meat or the occasional fur obtained in a raid. Even those who moved southward to the forests often made annual treks north to harvest the caribou migration—much to the dismay of their European trading partners. As always, the hallmark of the Chipewyans was flexibility and adaptability to the demands of the changing environment, ensuring that they would survive as a people for generations to come.

"Ambassadress of Peace," a 1953 illustration by artist Franklin Arbuckle, depicts Thanadeltur (center) negotiating a peace treaty between the Chipewyans and Crees.

THE LEGACY

OF

THANADELTUR

AND

MATONABBEE

While early European explorers failed to discover a Northwest Passage to Asia, they quickly discovered that it was possible to cross the upper half of North America east of the Rocky Mountains by canoe with relatively short portages. As more and more Europeans came to extract profit from the Great White North, they created competing markets for furs from indigenous groups. Seeking an advantage over the Hudson's Bay Company, traders from Montreal pressed inland by canoe in order to intercept bands of native traders on their way to the factories on the shoreline of Hudson Bay.

The increased number of European traders and fur markets brought about a burst in trade activity. Birch-bark canoe brigades traversed Canada's waterways with harvests of furs, while ships from Europe brought cargoes of guns, textiles, axes, and other trade goods to barter. The Chipewyans were increasingly drawn into these trade activities. Trading with the Montreal traders was enormously advantageous to them, allowing them to avoid the long journey to the Hudson Bay factories and to return to their families and their fur-hunting activities more quickly. The efforts of the Montreal traders were so successful that the profits of the Hudson's Bay Company were soon placed in serious danger.

But the Hudson's Bay Company was determined to prevent other European traders from undercutting their annual fur yield. By 1682 instructions to the factor were "to penetrate into the Countrey to make what discoveries you can, and to gett an Acquaintance and Commerce in the Indians thereabouts." To carry out these orders, the Hudson's Bay Company decided in 1715 to send its own expedition into the interior of Canada. Led by William Stuart, the expedition had the express purpose of contacting the Chipewyans and persuading them to increase their fur-trading activities directly with the company. The Stuart expedition left York Factory, located halfway up the west coast of Hudson Bay, on June 27, 1715. Its members included Stuart himself, 150 Cree members of the Hudson's Bay Company's home guard, and an approximately 20-year-old Chipewyan woman named Thanadeltur ("Marten Shake" in English). Thanadeltur was listed in Hudson's Bay Company records as simply an interpreter, but she was to have a vital role in the success of the mission.

As a teenager, Thanadeltur had been captured by a group of raiding Crees who had slaughtered all the men in her camp. Along with another Chipewyan girl, she had lived as a slave with her Cree captors. Thanadeltur and her fellow captive finally escaped the Crees, but her companion died in their bid for freedom. Although near starvation, Thanadeltur continued her daring escape, traveling down the Ten Shilling River to arrive at York Factory. There she quickly taught herself English, becoming the only person in York Factory who could speak Chipewyan, Cree, and English.

The Hudson's Bay factor at York Factory, James Knight, assigned Thanadeltur to the Stuart expedition because of her linguistic skills and her familiarity with both Chipewyan and Cree territory. Knight hoped that Thanadeltur could negotiate a peace between the feuding Chipewyans and Crees, who were embroiled in yet another territorial dispute that was distracting them from what Knight considered their essential fur-

trapping duties. Once peace had been established, Thanadeltur was to persuade the Chipewyans to engage in full-scale fur trade exclusively with the company. Knight's journal notes hopefully that Thanadeltur "will be of great Service to me in my Intention" of extending trade to the north. To aid her on her mission, Knight supplied Thanadeltur with a quantity of small trade goods as presents for the Chipewyans, and he promised that the Hudson's Bay Company would build a fort inland on the Churchill River to shorten the journey for the Chipewyans and help them avoid Cree territory.

But as the Stuart expedition set out across the Barren Grounds for the long and difficult northward trek to Chipewyan territory, it immediately ran into hardship. Beset by sickness and starvation, most of the Crees turned back to York Factory. The success of the mission was placed in even greater danger when the Stuart party came across the bodies of nine Chipewyans slain by another group of Crees. Fearful of retribution from the Chipewyans, the remaining Crees with Stuart insisted on turning back.

Thanadeltur somehow managed to persuade the party to camp for 10 days while she traveled alone and contacted her people further north. On the 10th day, as the Stuart party prepared to depart, Thanadeltur returned, accompanied by over 150 Chipewyans. Using her interpretive and persuasive abilities, she successfully negotiated a truce between the Chipewyans and the Crees, and the Stuart party, accompanied by 10 Chipewyan men, returned in triumph to the York

Factory on May 7, 1716—nearly a year after they had left. Stuart acknowledged that the success of his mission was entirely due to Thanadeltur, whom he called "the Chief promoter and Actor" of the truce. Knight was delighted with Thanadeltur's achievements and gave the Chipewyans who returned with her guns with which to hunt beaver. His journal states that he also "trained em up to the use of em. . . . Whereby they may Defend themselves if attacked by any of their Enemys."

Thanadeltur so impressed James Knight that he planned to send her along on another expedition into the interior. Thanadeltur had told Knight of other Native American bands who possessed a "yellow mettle," which Knight was certain was gold. Thanadeltur also described the terrain of a land far to the north, mentioning a broad strait through which great tides ebbed and flowed. Knight was certain that such a strait could only be the elusive Northwest Passage, a belief strengthened when he interrogated a group of Chipewyans who had come to York Factory to trade. The members of the group drew Knight a rough map of the territory to the north and assured him that some of the Chipewyans living there had spotted strange vessels on the water—vessels that Knight decided could be Japanese or Tartar ships at the western end of the Northwest Passage.

Knight began to organize another expedition to discover and claim the gold mines and the Northwest Passage, but his dream of vast riches was delayed when the annual supply ship from England failed to arrive at York Factory during the 1715–16 season—a failure that delayed Knight's plans to build a factory on the Churchill River as well. Thanadeltur and a group of Chipewyans, including her brother, remained at the York Factory, where she perfected her English and soon became an admired confidant of Knight, who constantly sought her advice in developing future plans for the company. But that winter Thanadeltur fell ill, and although Knight worked diligently to nurse her back to health, she died on February 5, 1717. Her death was a bitter blow to the factor, who had come to regard her as a friend. His journal records:

> I am about ready to break my heart.
> . . . She was one of a Very high Spirit
> and of the Firmest Resolution that
> ever I seen in any Body in my Days
> of great Courage and forecast.

Knight's dream of discovering riches to the north died soon after his friend. Determined to find the land Thanadeltur had described, Knight persuaded Hudson's Bay Company to back a major exploratory voyage. He embarked on two ships, the *Albany* and the *Discovery*. In 1722, Hudson's Bay Company books record the ships as "being castaway to the northward in Hudson's Bay," one of the growing list of arctic disasters in the European search for the Northwest Passage. The remains of the wreckage of the expedition were discovered nearly half a century later by Samuel Hearne, another Hudson's Bay Company explorer.

Hearne, an ambitious young former seaman and a diligent journal-keeper, was to have much of his destiny decided for him by the Chipewyans. Indeed, Hearne's expedition was organized in response to a large chunk of rich copper ore that some Chipewyans had brought to York Factory to trade during the mid-1760s. The chunk was transported by ex-

Hudson's Bay Company explorer Samuel Hearne was harassed, abandoned, and eventually adopted by the Chipewyans during his attempts to discover the Northwest Passage.

cited company men all the way to the company directors in London, who ordered an expedition "far to the north, to promote an extension of our trade, as well as for the discovery of a Northwest Passage [and] Copper Mines." The aspiring Hearne was chosen to lead this expedition through the Barren Grounds of Chipewyan territory, up the Coppermine River to the Arctic Ocean.

Hearne's first encounter with the Chipewyans was a disaster. As he set out with two other Europeans and a party of Crees from Fort Prince of Wales along Hudson Bay, a group of Chipewyans who had come to the factory to trade, led by a man known as Captain Chawchinahaw, departed along with him. After three weeks of northward travel, Chawchinahaw's party robbed Hearne and his company of their food stocks and supplies. The Crees accompanying Hearne quickly deserted him, and he and his two European companions had to travel the 200 miles back to Fort Prince of Wales alone and without provisions. Hearne and his men barely escaped starvation on their return journey, snaring rabbits and gnawing on the hides of their jackets for sustenance, but the experience opened Hearne's eyes to the survival value of native ways of life. Eventually, Hearne's acceptance of Chipewyan strategies for survival would enable him to penetrate deeper into the Barren Grounds than any European before him and to survive many harrowing ordeals.

In February of 1770, Hearne set off again, this time accompanied by an incompetent and dishonest Native Ameri-

FORT PRINCE OF WALES 1734

This illustration of Fort Prince of Wales in 1734 was taken from one of Hearne's engravings of the factory. The trading post was the birthplace of Hearne's Chipewyan guide and friend, Matonabbee.

can guide. By summer they had reached the Barren Grounds, where they joined a large band of Chipewyans. Hearne quickly ran out of trade goods, and as he was a poor hunter he soon became viewed as a burden by the band. As the cold weather of autumn set in, the Chipewyans stole Hearne's belongings and abandoned him with no snowshoes, tent, or warm clothes. Hearne, by this point without a guide and completely lost, began to attempt the long trek back to York Factory, but cold and hunger soon imperiled his life.

On September 20, 1770, Hearne, alone and near starvation, was found by a Chipewyan leader named Matonabbee. Fortunately for Hearne, Matonabbee, who was born at Fort Prince of Wales of a Cree slave woman and a Chipewyan hunter and was raised in part by a European, was as comfortable among Europeans as among Chipewyans. Matonabbee saved Hearne's life, giving him food and warm clothing and guiding him back to Fort Prince of Wales. During the journey back, Hearne told Matonabbee of his proposed expedition to the Arctic Ocean, and Matonabbee agreed to help him.

When Hearne slipped out from Fort Prince of Wales and joined Matonabbee, his eight wives, and his children a mere 12 days after his return, he joined his friend's band not as a fellow explorer but as a dependent and adoptive family member. While traveling with Matonabbee, Hearne entrusted his personal safety and the success of his mission to his status as a member of the powerful hunter's entourage—a considerably

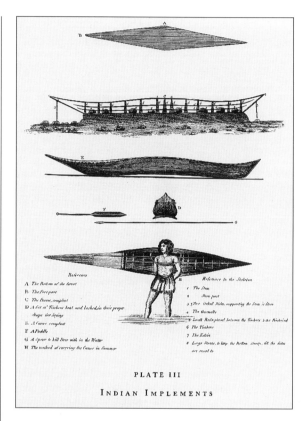

PLATE III

INDIAN IMPLEMENTS

An engraving from a 1796 published edition of Hearne's journals carefully blueprints some "Indian Implements"—a portable canoe and its paddles. The journals are one of the few existing records of 18th-century Chipewyan life.

more humble position than that of commander of an expedition. Hearne's humility was ultimately responsible for the success of his mission, both because Matonabbee's status protected Hearne from the harassment that had ended his previous expeditions, and because by following Matonabbee Hearne learned Chipewyan techniques for effectively living off the subarctic land. Fortunately for scholars, Hearne recorded all he learned of traditional Chipewyan habits, customs, and foods in great detail in his journals.

Hearne obviously admired Matonabbee, describing his "scrupulous adherence to truth and honesty that would have done honour to the most enlightened and devout Christian." But Matonabbee was in many ways more Chipewyan than European, and conflicts did arise, as when Matonabbee's party stopped on its way to the Arctic Ocean to slaughter a camp of Inuits. Hearne's disappointments continued when the party reached the Arctic Ocean on July 18, 1771, only to discover that both the Coppermine River leading into the ocean and the ocean channel itself were too shallow and rocky for ships to travel through. Hearne could only erect a marker claiming the Arctic Ocean shoreline for the Hudson's Bay Company and return home. On his last night in camp before reaching the fort, after a year and a half and 3,500 miles of travel, Hearne wrote in his journal:

> Though my discoveries are not likely to prove of any historical advantage to the Nation at large, nor indeed to the Hudson's Bay Company, yet I have had pleasure to think that I have fully complied with the orders of my Mentors, and that it has put a final end to all dispatches concerning a Northwest Passage through Hudson Bay.

Hearne's journey only temporarily laid to rest the Hudson's Bay Company's dreams of finding both the Northwest Passage and gold. But Hearne was to bequeath a more lasting legacy to scholars and explorers as the first European to explicitly acknowledge the superiority of Chipewyan survival techniques in the subarctic, and the first to follow (as well as to record) their traditional way of life.

Hearne's alliance with Matonabbee would also have lasting effects on the fur trade. In 1775, Matonabbee arrived at Fort Prince of Wales (where Hearne had been promoted to governor) with 300 companions and the largest Chipewyan fur haul in a century. While both Thanadeltur and Matonabbee's lives ended in tragedy (Matonabbee killed himself after French naval forces destroyed Fort Prince of Wales in 1782), they both helped establish the Chipewyans as major players in the fur trade of the Great White North—a legacy that has profoundly influenced Chipewyan history well into the present day.

A lithograph from the 1830s shows a Native American and a trader bartering for furs. By the late 18th century, many Chipewyans were heavily involved in the fur trade.

UNEQUAL
PARTNERS

Following Matonabbee's 1775 trading expedition, the southern Chipewyans quickly capitalized on their pivotal geographical position in the fur trade of the Great White North. Much as the Crees before them had done, they became both trappers and middlemen between the Europeans and other Athapaskan groups, using their traditional survival strategies and intimate knowledge of the terrain to venture where European trappers could not go, trekking into the interior to trade European goods to other indigenous groups at great profit.

While trade with the Hudson's Bay Company helped make the Chipewyans more powerful, the alliance between the traders and the Chipewyans was far from serene. Much like the Crees before them, the Chipewyans who were involved in the fur trade were always attempting to monopolize such trade. Hudson's Bay Company traders complained bitterly that Chipewyan hunters would intimi-

date weaker tribes into leaving the fur-bearing animals in their territory for the Chipewyans to hunt. Chipewyan traders would take advantage of the fact that prices for European goods were always cheaper at factories located on the shores of Hudson Bay than at factories located in the interior by purchasing goods on the bay, then traveling inland and selling the trade goods to other tribes for less than the inland factories would charge—a practice that infuriated the Europeans.

Worse yet was the fact that many Chipewyans still were not deeply involved in the fur trade and continued to hunt caribou in the Barren Grounds. With the cessation of hostilities with the Crees, a Chipewyan band living off caribou could easily survive with very little in the way of European goods. Hearne himself complained that

The real wants of these people are
few, and easily supplied; a hatchet,

an ice-chisel, a file and a knife, are
all that is required . . . to procure a
comfortable livelihood.

Chipewyan traditions surrounding death
created other problems for the Hudson's
Bay Company. If a Chipewyan hunter
died, any furs he had obtained were destroyed with all his other belongings. In
addition, if an epidemic or a series of
accidents killed enough members of a
band, the band would abandon an area,
even if it was rich with furs—and despite
the best efforts of the fur traders to end
this practice.

But despite these problems, the fur
trade was immensely profitable to the
Hudson's Bay Company—and much less
so to the Chipewyans. This was partly
due to the fact that trade with the Hudson's Bay Company was conducted in
terms of "made beaver," a term that originally referred to a pelt from an adult beaver in good condition, but that quickly
became its own sort of currency. Hudson's Bay Company account books were
kept in made beaver (often shortened to
MB); credit and debt were given in terms
of made beaver; and made-beaver exchange rates were regulated by the company much as the United States might
regulate the exchange rate of the dollar.
Indeed, even the design of the company's
famous trade blankets reflected the
made-beaver economy: the number of
black stripes along the edge of each blanket indicated how many made beaver the
blanket was worth.

Hudson's Bay Company records
kept at one post from 1822 to 1827 show
the average value for goods traded to

Native Americans in made beaver: a gun
was worth an average of 12.2 made beaver; a knife, 2.5 made beaver; a hat, 0.3
made beaver. The furs that the Native
Americans traded to the company were
also valued in made beaver: the average
muskrat pelt was worth 0.1 made beaver;
marten, 0.3 made beaver; lynx, 0.8 made
beaver; and beaver itself, 0.9 made beaver. As these exchange rates show, a Native American hunter would have to
trade in 122 muskrat pelts (more if they
were in poor condition or small) to buy a
single average gun—and the average
Hudson's Bay Company gun was a
cheaply made, notoriously unreliable
item. By charging high prices in pelts
(which were extremely valuable in
Europe) for inexpensive trade goods, the
Hudson's Bay Company was able to
make huge profits.

These profits were only as good as
the Hudson's Bay Company's monopoly
in the area, since other traders could easily undersell the company. Consequently,
much of the history of the Hudson's Bay
Company consists of its efforts (legal and
otherwise) to eliminate competition.
These efforts were for the most part quite
successful, and the company's control of
northern Canada was so complete that
up until the late 19th century the company was able to single-handedly prevent the common use of cash currency in
the region in an attempt to prevent Native American trappers from purchasing
goods from other companies.

Another method to ensure that hunters traded only with the Hudson's Bay
Company was the use of the credit sys-

Four Hudson's Bay Company made-beaver tokens, in increments ranging from ⅛ to 1 made beaver. Originally an adult beaver pelt in good condition, made beaver soon became a type of currency in northern Canada.

tem. Instead of simply exchanging goods for pelts when they were brought to the post, traders would issue such goods on credit to Chipewyan hunters at the beginning of each fur-hunting season. The goods were paid off in pelts when the Chipewyans returned to the post at the end of the season. Because each Chipewyan hunter owed a debt to a certain trading post, he was much more likely to trade at that post in the future and to spend the season hunting fur-bearing animals rather than food animals, resulting both in more pelts for the post and in

more incentive for the hunter to ask for goods—especially food—on credit the next year.

What made the credit system all the more appealing to the Hudson's Bay Company was that the trade goods taken on credit by Chipewyan hunters were so overpriced that even if a hunter only paid off a part of his debt, the company still made money. Indeed, company records show that by the late 1800s it had instituted a policy of discounting Native American debts by 25 percent. This meant that if a Native American hunter was forwarded 100 made beaver's worth of goods by a company trader, the debt was recorded in the account books as only being 75 made beaver, because 75 made beaver's worth of furs would cover the hunter's debt and the shipping and handling costs of the company as well as give the company an acceptable profit once it sold the furs on the open market. The Native Americans were kept unaware of this policy, however, so that the hunter in this transaction would believe that he had received 100 made beaver's worth of goods and was obligated to obtain 100 made beaver's worth of furs in order to remain in good standing at the post.

However unscrupulous these trading practices may seem, they paled in their deleterious effects when compared to the introduction of alcohol to the Chipewyans. Alcohol was brought to the tribe by fur traders at the end of the 18th century, when a group of independent traders formed the North West Company and began to compete fiercely with the Hudson's Bay Company for the Native American trade. The two companies vied with each other to provide goods that would sway the allegiance of native traders in their favor. One such good was a cheap and noxious alcoholic brew manufactured specifically for the Native American market. One common recipe for trade liquor called for one gallon of raw alcohol mixed with three gallons of water. To this base was added a pound of tea, a pound of black chewing tobacco, and a quart of black molasses to give it color and taste. A handful of red peppers

and a scoop of ginger added a kick that caused it to be christened "firewater." The Chipewyans had no experience with this intoxicating and addictive substance, and prodigious liquor consumption—invariably accompanied by increased violence and numerous accidents—created severe health problems.

Liquor availability was lessened somewhat after 1821, when the North West Company was taken over by the Hudson's Bay Company. The governor of the newly reorganized Hudson's Bay Company, George Simpson, attempted to bring about more orderly conditions now that the company had regained its fur trade monopoly, and he abolished the use of liquor as a trade good by the company. But bootleggers and unscrupulous traders could always smuggle some in, and to this day alcoholism remains a serious problem among North Canada's indigenous peoples.

Inadvertent imports brought by the European traders were diseases such as measles, influenza, and smallpox, which swept across the Great White North in a terrifying blizzard of sickness and death. The Chipewyans and other indigenous groups had no natural immunity against these European diseases, and traditional herbal remedies and the incantations and practices of inkonze proved useless. Entire camps would sicken, leaving no one in adequate physical condition to hunt or process food, and those who were not killed directly by disease would starve. Mortality rates were as high as 90 percent during some epidemics, and in the early 1820s, disease, combined with a trade

Canadian mounted police apprehend a whiskey trader as drunken Native Americans carouse in the background of this watercolor, painted by a Euro-Canadian wolf trapper. Alcohol continues to create a host of health problems for the indigenous peoples of northern Canada.

war against the neighboring Dogrib tribe, wiped out the entire Yellowknife division of the Chipewyan tribe. Disease continued to take a dreadful toll well into the 20th century.

The abandonment of the traditional caribou-hunting way of life and the introduction of the credit system, liquor, and the devastating new diseases of the Europeans brought social and cultural chaos to the Chipewyans. To many Chipewyans, the old ways—especially the old religious ways—simply did not seem sufficient to meet the new struggles that they now faced. Into this scene of religious and social chaos came a new force—Christianity. Many European Christian groups sought to claim native souls in the Great White North. These various groups

often competed against each other, seeking the greatest number of converts among indigenous peoples and racing north to reach new groups first. The winner of the race for the Chipewyans was easily the Roman Catholic Oblate Order of Mary Immaculate, which recruited missionaries primarily from the peasant population of southern France, where the order had been founded in 1814.

In 1845, Abbé Thibault of the Oblate Order made contact with the Chipewyans. His reception was a warm one, and by the next year Oblate priests were creating a written form of the Chipewyan language to better communicate with the tribe. Soon after, an Oblate priest named Father Laflèche wrote a Chipewyan grammar, and a Chipewyan convert named Joseph Touzae taught his fellow tribespeople to read. In 1852 a group of northern Chipewyans who traded at Fort Resolution on the southeast shore of Great Slave Lake invited an Oblate missionary, Father Faraud, to work among them. Father Faraud was supported by a prominent Métis leader named Pierre Beaulieu and was assisted by a Chipewyan man named Denegonusye, who helped Faraud convert over 300 Chipewyans to the Roman Catholic faith, earning himself a new name, Yaltyiyazi, or "Little Father."

The Oblate missionaries were impressed by the enthusiasm of the Chipewyans for Christianity; one described tribe members as being "trusting in what one tells them and desirous to live well." But this enthusiasm reflected in great part the Chipewyans' traditional belief in inkonze. The Oblates and other Europeans seemed immune to the many new diseases that had devastated the Chipewyans, and since the Chipewyans believed that diseases were caused by spells, this was seen as an indication that the Europeans had a new and powerful form of inkonze. In addition, many Chipewyans accepted the missionaries because they could obtain trade goods for their followers (although, like all Europeans in their territory, the missionaries initially depended on the Chipewyans for food and shelter). While such converts were cynically dubbed "Tobacco Christians" by Europeans, the Chipewyans viewed the material wealth of the missionaries as a bona fide miracle. Missionaries had only to send a bit of

paper across the water to Europe and a ship would arrive with trade goods for them—strong inkonze indeed!

In 1857 the Oblate missionaries were joined by the Sisters of Charity of Montreal, also known as the Grey Nuns, who staffed hospitals, schools, and orphanages and founded many convents. The convents soon proved necessary when the missionaries condemned polygamy and made it clear that Christian converts would be expected to cast off all but one wife. The responsibility of supporting the "extra" wives shed by converts quickly became that of the Grey Nuns.

In 1861 Bishop Vital J. Grandin established a permanent Oblate mission at Fort Providence, which soon became the base for a rapid expansion of missionary activities to the north. One of the most famous Oblates to come through this mission during the 19th century was Father Emile Petitot, whom the Chipewyans called Yaltei-Deg-Ceze, "the egg-shaped one," on account of his portliness. Father Petitot had a genuine respect for the civilization of the Chipewyan and other northern tribes, and he felt that the key to success in missionary work was to learn the language, customs, and beliefs of each group completely. He began to compile a French-Chipewyan dictionary and to record Chipewyan myths and legends as both a missionary and an ethnographic effort, and much of the recorded material concerning Chipewyan culture in the 19th century is the result of Father Petitot's efforts.

Due to the efforts of the Oblates and the Grey Nuns, most of the Chipewyans eventually converted to Roman Catholicism. These converts, however, usually viewed the new religion as a supplement to, not a replacement for, their traditional beliefs, and they combined the practices of the new religion with those of the old. This mixing of religious beliefs was unacceptable to the missionaries, who believed that the Chipewyans had to give up all aspects of their traditional religions and many aspects of their traditional life in order to save their souls from perdition. Missionaries began distributing rosaries, religious medals, and portable statues to Chipewyan hunters and traders to replace the traditional rituals and taboos surrounding such expeditions. To demonstrate the supernatural favor they enjoyed, missionaries would wow observers by utilizing new gadgets or predicting natural phenomena such as eclipses. Missionaries also sponsored public processions and celebrations on various religious holidays—large communal gatherings of many bands that eventually took on many of the same social functions as the communal caribou hunts and summer fishing camps. Since the Oblate missionaries were French, certain aspects of French culture were adopted by the Chipewyans, including the taking of French names and the traditional French hostility toward Germans, who eventually joined the Chipewyan pantheon of threatening bushmen. In addition, Roman Catholic prohibitions on divorce were strongly (and somewhat maniacally) emphasized by the Oblate missionaries, to the extent that ending a marriage

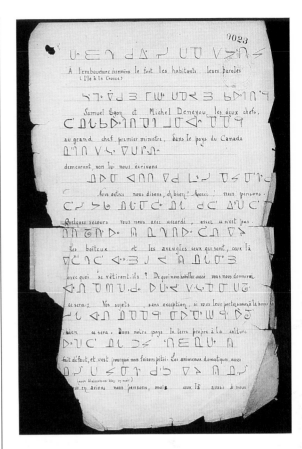

The first page of a three-page letter, dated July 28, 1883, written in Chipewyan by two tribal leaders to a Canadian governmental official (a French translation has been added by a local Catholic bishop). The Chipewyan alphabet was created and refined by Oblate missionaries.

for any reason became unacceptable among tribe members.

While the missionaries did affect Chipewyan culture, their attempts to entirely replace traditional Chipewyan beliefs and culture were met with a good

A beaver pelt stretches on a frame in preparation for trade. The attempts of the Oblates to end the Chipewyan involvement in the fur trade created a great deal of friction between the missionaries and the traders.

deal of alarm, both by the tribe and by the European fur traders. It was commonly believed by the missionaries that Christianization would work only in a sedentary society, one that was based upon the ordered seasons of farming, that would allow children to attend school, and that would allow all members of the community to receive the benefits of regular religious worship and rituals. Consequently, the missionaries agitated for the abolition of the fur trade and its replacement by farming. (The impracticality of attempting agricultural projects in a subarctic environment did not dissuade the missionaries from what they viewed as the correct spiritual path.) For European fur traders, whose livelihood was dependent upon the continuation of Chipewyan involvement in the fur trade, the missionaries' plans spelled the end of their own way of life as well as that of the tribe, and the two groups found themselves in conflict.

The missionaries' willingness to dictate the way in which the Chipewyans should live was due in part to their belief that not only was European Christianity a better religion than traditional Chipewyan beliefs, but that white European Christians were an intellectually, morally, and culturally superior people to the Native Americans. Many theories were propounded during the 19th century to "explain" this superiority; one such idea that was popular among many of the Oblates working with the Chipewyans was the idea of degeneration. This theory held that humans had been created in perfection by the Christian God, but when they were evicted from the Garden of Eden they had begun to degenerate, becoming dumber, smaller, weaker, and more savage. The only way to stop this degeneration was to accept Christianity; those groups that had not yet accepted this religion or had accepted it recently were far more degenerated than the fortunate Europeans, who had been practicing Christianity for centuries. Even the relatively enlightened Father Petitot subscribed firmly to this belief, arguing that the Chipewyans and other Native Americans in Canada's north were "some lost remnants of Israel now converted to Catholicism . . . [but] sullied by the fetishism of shamanism."

The notion that the Chipewyans were somehow "sullied" provided a convenient rationale for excluding them from positions of religious authority. Although there were many Chipewyan converts to Roman Catholicism, the office of priest was the privilege of the Europeans, and all the most devout Chipewyans could hope for was to serve as *dogiques,* who ensured that other Chipewyans adhered to church rules but who lacked power within the Catholic religious hierarchy. This pattern of unequal partnership between the European fur traders and missionaries and the Chipewyans was to be continued with the next group of Europeans the Chipewyans encountered— government officials.

A Chipewyan chief sits flanked by two councillors in this 1910 photograph. The men are draped in a British flag and wear medals bearing the likeness of King Edward VII of England.

THE
BIG
THREE

The Chipewyans had been masters of survival in the subarctic for millennia, but as the modern era approached they no longer seemed in control of their own destiny. Traders, missionaries, and government officials would repeatedly attempt to determine the future of the Chipewyans. This triumvirate of nonnative powers, popularly known as "The Big Three," held Canada's north in a paternalistic grasp that seemed unbreakable to a people who were not prepared culturally, economically, or politically to understand and exploit the workings of Western organizations and laws. The Chipewyans were buffeted by the winds of change in a landscape that no longer held the bounty or security of the past.

In 1870, the Dominion of Canada purchased the territories of the Hudson's Bay Company for £300,000. This land transfer brought under Canadian sovereignty all of Alberta and Saskatchewan, most of Manitoba, two-thirds of present-day Ontario and Quebec including what is now mainland Newfoundland (Labrador), and the area which is known today as the Northwest Territories. In addition, the transfer signaled the end of an economic and social system that had been underpinned by the fur trade. Although the Chipewyans would continue to hunt and trap, the importance of the fur trade in Chipewyan life would gradually be eclipsed by a new authority—the government of Canada.

In the years preceding the creation of the nation of Canada in 1867, the British government had handled relations with the various Native American tribes through the Indian Department of its Colonial Office. The British had viewed the Chipewyans and other tribes almost exclusively as potential allies in battle, first against the French, and later against the Americans. Consequently, the primary interactions between the British authorities and the Chipewyans were a series of annual ceremonies sponsored by the British at which presents and medals were distributed to reward loyalty and good behavior. Such ceremonies were fairly superficial and brief, and the Chipewyans had a much more familiar and complex relationship with the representatives of the Hudson's Bay Company than they did with the representatives of the British Crown.

The Canadian government sought to change all this. In 1876 the Canadian Parliament created the Department of Indian Affairs to oversee the government's interactions with Native Americans. A major goal of the department was to acquire territory from the various tribes. Toward that end, the Canadian government began to make a series of numbered treaties with various tribes. Initially these treaties did not affect northern Canada, which was considered worthless for settlement by the Canadians. But during the early 1880s, the Geological and Natural History Survey of Canada began dispatching surveyors into the northern territory. The surveyors discovered rich deposits of oil, gold, silver, copper, and uranium, and the image of the north changed overnight from that of a wasteland to that of a land of incredible opportunity.

Canada quickly moved to consolidate control over the north, carving up the area in a series of five treaties, numbers 7 through 11, between 1897 and 1922. These treaties gave the government half the area of present-day Canada in exchange for small amounts of money, presents of medals, flags, equipment for fishing and hunting, and an annual payment for each individual who came under the jurisdiction of the treaties. Members of tribes who signed such treaties became known as treaty or status Indians; one such tribe was the Chipewyans, who came under the province of two of the five treaties, number 8 of 1899–1900 and number 10 of 1906–7.

Although the Canadian government eagerly accepted the validity of treaties number 8 and 10, serious questions have been raised concerning their legality. Most Chipewyans at this time did not speak English, and treaty negotiations were conducted with the use of Chipewyan translators, whose own grasp of English may not have been that strong. Much was assuredly lost in the cultural translation as well, since a number of Western legal and political concepts that informed the treaty were completely foreign to the Chipewyans. For example, the text of treaty number 8 is a fairly straightforward (to Westerners) surrender of territory and sovereignty that reads in part:

> Whereas, the said Commissioners have proceeded to negotiate a treaty with the Cree, Beaver, Chipewyan and other Indians, inhabiting the district hereinafter defined and described, and the same has been agreed upon and concluded by the respective bands at the dates mentioned hereunder, the said Indians DO HEREBY CEDE, RELEASE, SURRENDER AND YIELD UP to the Government of the Dominion of Canada, for Her Majesty the Queen and Her successors for ever, all their rights, titles and privileges whatsoever, to the lands included within the following limits. . . .

And Her Majesty the Queen HEREBY AGREES with the said Indians that they shall have right to pursue their usual vocations of hunting, trapping and fishing throughout the tract surrendered as heretofore described, subject to such regulations as may from time to time be made by the Government of the country, acting under the authority of Her Majesty, and saving and excepting such tracts as may be required or taken up from time to time for settlement, mining, lumbering, trading or other purposes.

To the Chipewyans, the above passages contradicted each other, because title to land in Chipewyan society meant the right to use the land and its resources and to range freely over the territory. Consequently, giving up ownership of the land while not giving up the right to use that land was a wholly nonsensical notion to them. The Chipewyans apparently repeatedly expressed concern about their right to use the land; these concerns could have been interpreted as the equivalent to objecting to giving up ownership of the land, but they were never construed that way by Canadian authorities. The Report of the Commissioners states:

There was expressed at every point the fear that the making of the treaty would be followed by the curtailment of their hunting and fishing privileges. . . . We assured them that the treaty would not lead to any forced interference with their mode of life.

Although it is almost certain that the Chipewyans had doubts about the treaty,

This medal, issued in 1907 to commemorate the signing of Treaty Number 10, is engraved with a representation of a treaty commissioner shaking hands with a stereotypically (and considering the weather in the area covered by the treaty, woefully inadequately) clad Native American chief.

the missionaries supported signing, which was apparently enough to convince the tribe to put faith in the government representatives.

In addition to the cultural confusion, interviews with Chipewyans and others present at the signing of the treaty have cast a great deal of doubt on the legality of the conduct of the Canadian officials involved. For example, an examination of oral histories shows that many of the supposed chiefs at the signing of treaties were appointed on the spot by government agents, much as Hudson's Bay Company traders had appointed trading chiefs in the past. The agents certainly did not treat these appointed chiefs as men with authority; one of the men designated as chief by agents during the signing of treaty number 8 resigned in disgust when the agents would not listen to his suggestions or answer his questions.

Questions have been raised concerning the honesty of the Canadians' representation of the treaty. Pierre Mercredi, an interpreter for the Chipewyans at the signing of treaty number 8, recalled:

> I interpreted the words of Queen Victoria to Alexandre Laviolette, Chief of the Chipewyan and his band. . . . I know, because I read the Treaty to them, that there was no clause in it which said they might have to obey regulations about hunting. They left us no copy of the Treaty we signed, saying that they would have it printed and send a copy to us. When the copy came back, that second clause was in it. It was not there before. I never read it to the Chipewyan or explained it to them. I have no doubt that the new regulation breaks that old treaty.

Another Chipewyan man, Johnny Jean Marie Beaulieu, who was interviewed for a Chipewyan oral history, gave this narration of the Canadian explanation of the treaty:

And the Indian Agent said, "As long as the sun shines and the rivers flow this is your land to hunt on forever. . . . This land is yours. As long as we pay the treaty [i.e. pay annual treaty benefits], nothing is going to change". . . . "If this is so, we will take the treaty," the Chiefs said.

And a Chipewyan man named Antoine Beaulieu, who was 16 years old when treaty number 8 was signed at Smith's Landing on July 15, 1899, recalled:

> What I understood then was that they won't stop us from killing anything and there won't be no law against anything, game and so on. . . . They said if you take this money you will never be in trouble or hard up or anything if you take this money . . . all they done was had some talk then paid out the treaty. . . . In one day it was all over.

Even the legitimacy of the signatures on treaty number 8 has been called into question. Since many of the chiefs could neither read nor write, they acknowledged their agreement by marking an X on the treaty. Some of these Xs are in a different color ink than the others and seem to have been made by a single person, bringing up the possibility that they were forged by a government official.

After the treaties were signed the Canadian government immediately made its presence felt by regulating trapping. The government set aside areas for wildlife sanctuaries, beaver conservation areas, and registered trapline areas without taking into account local traditions of land tenure. Each type of district had its

A Native American fur trapper trades at a Hudson's Bay Company store in the early 1900s. After the purchase of the company's territory in 1870, the Canadian government effectively ended the company's monopoly on the Chipewyan fur trade.

own set of rules and regulations, resulting in a bewildering onslaught of bureaucracy that further served to alienate and anger the Chipewyans. New government regulations decreed the number of caribou the Chipewyans could kill to feed their families and the number of beaver pelts they could trade for supplies, and the North West Mounted Police (later the Royal Canadian Mounted Police), introduced to the area in 1900, were distressingly efficient in enforcing what the Chipewyans viewed as capricious and provocative regulations. At the same time, the land rights of Native Americans in northern Canada were steadily being eroded as Euro-Canadian development crept northward in the Ca-

A group of Chipewyans land at Fort Resolution on the shores of the Great Slave Lake in what is now the Northwest Territories. Annual treaty conventions in towns such as Fort Resolution attracted hundreds of Chipewyans from the surrounding areas

nadian Shield, destroying trapping and hunting areas that were supposedly protected by the treaties. Resistance to Canadian authorities by the various tribes became increasingly common.

In order to maintain control of the area, the Canadian government dispatched officials called commissioners throughout the north. The commissioners traveled through each territory by boat, met with the various indigenous groups, and, in perhaps the ultimate testament to the confusion surrounding the treaties, explained the content of the treaties to each tribe. The presence of the commissioners placed the Oblate missionaries living among the Chipewyans in a peculiar role. Many of the commis-

sioners and other government agents dealing with the Native Americans came directly from Europe and were usually completely ignorant of the indigenous cultures and languages of Canada (and sometimes unfamiliar with Canadian law as well). Consequently, the government enlisted the missionaries already present in each area to act as interpreters and negotiators. Although the Oblate missionaries maintained their earlier practice of encouraging the Chipewyans to become settled farmers (an idea also embraced by governmental representatives), they now found themselves defending and explaining Chipewyan customs and way of life to outsiders, and they soon began to actively defend

Chipewyan interests during negotiations with the Canadian government. Both Oblates and Chipewyans, however, found the Canadian government almost wholly unresponsive to Chipewyan demands and concerns.

Although during this time the Canadian government failed to provide the Native Americans of northern Canada with the protection, medical assistance, and education regularly received by southern Canadians, it did give out annual treaty benefits, consisting of cash and goods. The introduction of cash to the region, combined with the construction of the Canadian Pacific Railroad to the south of Chipewyan territory, helped open the area to more businesses and trade operations, destroying the Hudson's Bay Company's trade monopoly. The end of the company's dominance in the area had the ironic effect of increasing Chipewyan involvement in the fur trade. Competition among traders drastically lowered prices for Euro-Canadian goods, including foodstuffs, and increased prices for furs; at the same time, the introduction of cash currency meant that Chipewyans could shop around for the best prices. Trapping became much more lucrative, and by the 1910s even the more traditional northern Chipewyans had settled into small villages (although they still made seasonal hunting migrations), were engaged in trapping, and were partially dependent on trade for food.

The end of the Hudson's Bay Company's monopoly also eliminated the need for trading chiefs who would nego-tiate trade deals; instead, each trapper could pick and choose among competing bids for his furs. Negotiations with the Canadian government took on new importance, however, and this became the duty of the chiefs appointed by the government during the treaty signings (their prestige was increased by the fact that their status meant they received larger annual benefits). In keeping with the Chipewyan tradition of limited political authority, such chiefs were viewed merely as spokesmen for their group, not as commanders or representatives for the entire tribe.

As trade expanded, the old Hudson's Bay Company factories were transformed into bona fide towns, with stores, government offices, and many residents, especially elderly Chipewyans who could no longer endure the rigors of hunting and trapping. These towns gained importance as the sites of the annual treaty conventions, where the Chipewyans and Canadians would supposedly renew their commitment to the treaties by engaging in negotiations (often fruitless by Chipewyan standards) and by the payment and acceptance of the annual treaty benefits (which were occasionally refused by disgruntled tribe members). The conventions, which occurred in the summer, drew in hundreds of Chipewyans from the surrounding regions and became an important time to socialize with distant friends and relations, share grievances against the Canadian authorities, arrange marriages, and celebrate a common identity.

This 1990 photo captures three Chipewyan children—(front to back) Jamie Sanderson, K'ai Catholique, and Pekecho Lockhart—drawing on the chalkboard in a classroom in the town of Lutsel k'e (formerly known as Snowdrift) located in the Northwest Territories. During the 1960s and 1970s, the Chipewyans organized to effect major reforms in education.

AT
THE
CROSSROADS

While the Canadian government had played an essential role in breaking the monopoly of the Hudson's Bay Company, its unwillingness to provide basic medical and educational services soon created serious problems. European-introduced diseases continued to sweep the north and spread all the more quickly due to improved transportation and the periodic large Chipewyan gatherings for religious holidays and treaty payments. For example, in 1928 influenza was inadvertently spread to the entire Chipewyan tribe in under 24 hours by a Hudson's Bay Company ship that was visiting the various regional treaty conventions, and the resulting epidemic killed between one-fifth and one-fourth of the Chipewyan population.

In the absence of effective government care, the missionaries and the Hudson's Bay Company tried to provide vaccinations for the population and act as dispensaries for medicines, but they had few people and little money to spread over a population that covered a vast territory. The health situation of the Chipewyans gradually improved in the 1930s and 1940s as the missionaries and Hudson's Bay Company traders pressured the Canadian government to provide better health care and as many Chipewyans moved permanently into the larger towns, where they were closer to medical facilities.

The provision of education was also stipulated in the treaties, but once again the Canadian government chose to rely on the missionaries to provide education for the Chipewyans. Children were sent off to missionary-run boarding schools that were infamous for their bad food and severe discipline. The schools were seriously underfunded and were forced to be self-sufficient; consequently, Chipewyan students spent so much time raising food and doing chores that very few of them had the time to learn how to read and write. While mission schools did bring together Chipewyan children from various regions and inadvertently helped forge a stronger tribal identity, the schools also denigrated Chipewyan traditions. Schoolchildren learned to dislike "savage" conditions such as being dirty or eating with the hands, which are unavoidable while hunting and trapping, and parents often felt that their children had been spoiled for Chipewyan life but had not been taught the skills necessary to succeed in Euro-Canadian society.

Most Chipewyan children who went to school between 1920 and 1950 never went beyond the fifth or sixth grade, and adult education was totally neglected. This was true for other tribes as well as the Chipewyans—most Native American adults did not even receive rudimentary instruction in the workings of the fur trade or the system of Canadian government. And although the government stressed plans for vocational training for mining, gas, oil, and other industries based upon northern Canada's natural resources, by 1939 not one Native American was employed in these occupations.

While fur prices remained high and fur trapping remained a fairly lucrative business from the late 1910s to the mid-1930s, the global economic depression of the 1930s lowered fur prices significantly, causing serious hardships for the Chipewyans. These hardships were compounded by a decline in the population of fur-bearing animals caused by overtrapping, which became a problem as more and more Euro-Canadian trappers moved into the area. Euro-Canadian

trappers were usually transients who simply wanted to get as much money from the fur trade as possible and then return to the south. Consequently, they often picked an area rich in fur-bearing animals, trapped out the entire animal population, and then moved on to the next region. (The Chipewyans did not trap nearly as intently as the whites because they saw trapping as a supplement to their primary food-gathering activities of hunting and fishing.) The population of fur-bearing animals plummeted, and the Canadian government was forced to act, banning non-local trappers from the Northwest Territories in 1938.

But banning transient trappers did not help the decline in fur prices, nor did it help when a series of devastating forest fires seriously reduced the caribou population after World War II. In addition, many of the new developments brought by Euro-Canadians resulted in the clearing of land, destroying a great deal of prime wildlife habitat. Tailings from mines poisoned lakes and streams, rendering fish unsafe for consumption. The developments employed many Euro-Canadians from Canada's more urban south; these people were often unaware that others made their living from the wilderness, and they would carelessly destroy Chipewyan traplines and fishing nets while pleasure boating.

As living off the land became more difficult and as industries such as mines, fisheries, and sawmills sprouted up outside of the larger Canadian North towns, more and more Chipewyans moved permanently to towns, abandoning any sort

This photograph, taken sometime during the 1920s, shows a Chipewyan trading a pelt for a gun. Fur trapping was especially profitable from the late 1910s to the mid-1930s.

of seasonal travel. This trend was accelerated when the Canadian government finally began to provide extensive services to the Chipewyans in the 1940s and 1950s. Improved town schools impelled families to settle permanently so that their children could attend school. Social assistance programs such as welfare, old-age, and disability benefits hastened the settlement of towns because checks had to be picked up each month and because people were assured of an adequate income without hunting or otherwise living off the land. The trapping and hunting that did occur ceased being a family affair; a trapper's wife and chil-

dren would stay in town to attend school and collect welfare while the trapper (usually in partnership with another trapper or two) absented himself for a month or more to hunt and obtain furs. But it was not easy for a trapper to be separated from his family for that long, and when fur prices were low many men simply stayed at home.

Idleness and unemployment, combined with easy access to trade goods, resulted in high rates of alcoholism among the Chipewyans, as well as diet-related medical disorders such as obesity, diabetes, and tooth decay. Adding to these problems was a profound feeling of political disempowerment that was barely alleviated when registered Indians received the federal vote in 1953. For decades, the Chipewyans had had their concerns ignored by the Canadian government—so much so that elections held to choose a spokesperson to voice Chipewyan concerns to the Canadian government were viewed as a joke and almost no one would vote. Chipewyan society had never had large-scale or complex political organizations, and a fragmented and relatively small Chipewyan population could not make its voice heard in Canadian national politics. Chipewyans living in towns rarely felt that they were living in a community, and they tended to allow the Euro-Canadian population of the town (which was usually small, transient, and unfamiliar with Chipewyan traditions) to dominate the local government.

Perhaps the saddest instance of Euro-Canadian domination of Chipewyan affairs occurred in 1957, when a Chipewyan band located at Duck Lake in Saskatchewan Province was removed to the town of Churchill on Hudson Bay. The shift from living in small, Chipewyan-dominated settlements in the woods to living in what the Canadian government later admitted was a crime-ridden slum proved too much for most band members, and in 1971 some 70 to 80 band members returned to their former territory and lifestyle.

The political domination of the Chipewyans began to change in 1969 when Minister of Indian Affairs Jean Chrétien offered a "Statement of the Government of Canada on Indian Policy" to the Canadian House of Commons. This "White Paper," as a government publication printed for the information of Parliament is known, addressed criticisms of the paternalistic nature of Canadian Indian administration. The propositions put forth in the White Paper were radical, calling for the abolition of both the existing special benefits for treaty Indians and the Department of Indian Affairs. Further, the White Paper called for the transfer of control of Indian lands to the Native Americans themselves.

Implementation of the proposals outlined in the White Paper would have transferred responsibility for Native American affairs to the provincial governments. It also would have meant that the Chipewyans and other tribes would never gain full recognition by the Canadian government of their status as indigenous peoples and would lose any special protection of their territory. The response to the White Paper from the Chipewyans and other indigenous groups throughout Canada was overwhelmingly negative. But the outrage that greeted Chrétien's suggestions sparked a renewed interest in the subject of Indian policy and affairs among both the indigenous and Euro-Canadian populations.

The White Paper was a catalyst for the Chipewyans and other indigenous peoples to organize politically. One result of this organization was a re-examination of the circumstances surrounding the original treaty agreements between the Canadian government and the Chipewy-

Jean Chrétien (in sweater), who as Canadian Minister of Indian Affairs proposed the controversial 1969 "Statement of the Government of Canada on Indian Policy."

ans. Beginning in 1966, the Indian Brotherhood of the North West Territory and the Company of Young Canadians conducted tape-recorded interviews of Native Americans who were present at the signing of treaties, preserving and disseminating the Chipewyan view of the treaty agreements.

But the primary goal of Chipewyan political organization was the right to self-determination and autonomy in resolving issues concerning the environment, land rights, welfare, education, and economic development. Chipewyans also began to realize that their grievances were shared with other Native American tribes, and soon activists from many tribes began working together.

When during the 1970s the Canadian government sought to construct a pipeline to extract natural gas and oil in the Mackenzie Valley, the Beaufort Sea, and the High Arctic, the Chipewyans responded quickly with steps to protect their lands and rights. Along with other peoples of the north they banded together to form the Dene Nation, which they referred to as "the Fourth World," a domestic colony within the borders of Canada. They demanded self-determination, rights to their traditional lands, and special status under the Canadian Constitution, and passed the following declaration on July 19, 1975:

> We the Dene of the Northwest Territories insist on the right to be regarded by ourselves and the world as a nation.
>
> Our struggle is for the recognition of the Dene Nation by the Government and peoples of Canada and the peoples and the governments of the world. . . .
>
> What we seek then is independence and self determination within the country of Canada. This is what we mean when we call for a just land settlement for the Dene nation.

The formation of the Dene Nation and its strong opposition to the proposed gas developments prompted the Canadian government to place a 10-year moratorium on any such developments in the Northwest Territories. But the Dene Nation was not a single-issue organization, and on October 25, 1976, the nation proposed a new agreement between themselves and the Canadian government that would supersede previous treaties and recognize their right to self-determination. The agreement called for the Dene to participate with Euro-Canadians as equal partners, reading in part:

> The lessons of the Treaties and the lesson of our experience since that time is that our rights will not be adequately protected by assurances of non-Dene institutions, be they corporations or the Federal Government. Our rights will only be protected by the assertion of those rights by ourselves.

Such political organization has helped the Chipewyans to address issues directly affecting their communities, and members of the Dene Nation have spoken on national and international levels concerning environmental policy in northern Canada. For example, Chipewyan and Cree leaders have called for Canada's federal and provincial governments to monitor the industrial pollution endangering the Athabasca Delta and the water supplies of local Native American communities.

While they are concerned about wilderness preservation, members of the Dene Nation have criticized environmental groups based in southern Canada that have sought stricter hunting and trapping regulations. These regulations would wreak havoc on the livelihoods of Native Americans. Bill Erasmus, president of the Dene Nation, has pointed out that the Native Americans who live in northern Canada "know the capacity of the land" and have a considerably more intimate knowledge of its resources than groups based hundreds of miles to the south. The Dene Nation has also criticized the stand taken against wearing fur by some environmental groups. Canada's 1.5 million indigenous citizens pro-

Chipewyan fisherman (and local health center employee) Louie Abel exhibits his catch, taken from the Great Slave Lake. Sound environmental policy is a serious concern for many Chipewyans, who obtain or supplement their incomes by hunting or fishing.

A group of Chipewyan children display the fruits of a cranberry-picking expedition. Future generations will ultimately determine the relationship between the Chipewyan people and the Canadian government.

vide one-fourth of the fur that is exported from the country each year, and the success of the anti-fur campaign would destroy an important source of their income.

Changes have also occurred in education. Most of the missionary-run residential schools were closed by the end of the 1970s, and in 1991 Reverend Doug Crosby, president of the Oblate Conference of Canada, delivered an apology during a religious pilgrimage to Lac Ste. Anne for past hostility of the order's schools to-

ward Chipewyan culture and religion. The speech, translated into Chipewyan and Cree, asked for "forgiveness and understanding" from the listeners and stated:

> We recognize, in spite of their efforts and in spite of the goodness of their efforts, the residential schools have caused pain for many . . . that they have left deep scars in some of the former students.

Today, education is seen as a means of teaching Chipewyan children about their own rich culture. Children in early grades are often taught in their native language, and there are programs designed to attract native teachers to the classroom. To ensure cultural sensitivity, the Chipewyans have also demanded a voice in curriculum development and teacher training.

The Chipewyans have become teachers in turn, teaching fellow Canadians about northern Canada's indigenous heritage. One example is the Prince of Wales Northern Heritage Center in Yellowknife, where a multicultural and multilingual staff runs a variety of exhibitions, artifacts, and records. Special Heritage Advisors work with community museums and heritage groups across northern Canada to help them document and preserve their unique local history. One result of these efforts is that Chipewyan place names are now being recognized by the Canadian government and public. For example, one Chipewyan settlement on the southern shore of the eastern arm of Great Slave Lake was known by Canadians as Snowdrift but is now officially *Lutsel k'e,* a Chipewyan name meaning "the place of small fish."

Today the Chipewyans are at a cultural and political crossroad. Some Chipewyans feel that tribal members must further integrate into mainstream Canadian society in order to be considered on an equal footing with their southern neighbors. Others argue that integration into Canadian society is paramount to the loss of their unique cultural identity. Most likely elements from both schools of thought will be incorporated into a way of life that is uniquely Chipewyan in outlook and composition. As the Chipewyans once calculated ice, wind, and wildlife conditions to make decisions for the survival of their people, today they must calculate the costs and benefits of assimilation and segregation in a modern Canada.

BIBLIOGRAPHY

Clark, Annette McFayden, ed. *Northern Athapaskan Conference Proceedings, 1971.* Ottawa: Canadian Ethnology Service, 1975.

Crowe, Keith J. *A History of the Original Peoples of Northern Canada.* Montreal: McGill-Queens University Press, 1991.

Dickerson, Mark O. *Whose North? Political Change, Political Development, and Self-Government in the Northwest Territories.* Vancouver: University of British Columbia Press, 1992.

Fumoleau, René. *As Long as This Land Shall Last: A History of Treaty 8 and Treaty 11, 1870–1939.* Toronto: McClelland and Steward Limited, 1973.

Grant, John Webster. *Moon of Wintertime: Missionaries and Indians of Canada in Encounter Since 1534.* Toronto: University of Toronto Press, 1984.

Newman, Peter C. *Empire of the Bay: An Illustrated History of the Hudson's Bay Company.* Toronto: Madison Press Books, 1989.

Sharp, Henry S. *The Transformation of Bigfoot: Maleness, Power, and Belief Among the Chipewyan.* Washington, D.C.: Smithsonian Institution Press, 1988.

Smith, David Merrill. *Inkonze: Magico-Religious Beliefs of Contact-Traditional Chipewyan Trading at Fort Resolution, NWT, Canada.* Ottawa: National Museums of Canada, 1973.

Smith, J. G. E. "The Chipewyan." In *Subarctic: Handbook of North American Indians,* edited by J. Helm. Vol. 6. Washington, D.C.: Smithsonian Institution Press, 1981.

Symington, Fraser. *The Canadian Indian: The Illustrated History of the Great Tribes of Canada.* Toronto: McClelland & Stewart, 1969.

Van Stone, James W. *Athapaskan Adaptations: Hunters and Fishermen of the Subarctic Forests.* Chicago: Aldine Publishing, 1974.

Watkins, Mel, ed. *Dene Nation: The Colony Within.* Toronto: University of Toronto Press, 1977.

Yerbury, C. *The Subarctic Indians and the Fur Trade, 1680–1860.* Vancouver: University of British Columbia Press, 1986.

THE CHIPEWYAN AT A GLANCE

TRIBE *Chipewyan*
CULTURE AREA *Subarctic*
GEOGRAPHY *Alberta, Saskatchewan, Manitoba, Northwest Territories (Mackenzie and Keewatin districts)*
LINGUISTIC FAMILY *Athapaskan*
CURRENT POPULATION *Approximately 5,000*
FEDERAL STATUS *Recognized as "Status Indians" under the Federal Indian Act.*

GLOSSARY

Algonquin A group of linguistically related Native American tribes who inhabited an area ranging from what is now southern Canada to the southern United States.

anthropologist A scientist who studies human beings and their culture.

Athapaskan Among Native Americans, the most widely dispersed linguistic family. Athapaskan speakers such as the Chipewyans can be found not only in Canada but also along the Northwest Coast, in Alaska, and in the American Southwest.

babiche Semi-tanned caribou or moose hide, usually cut into long strips and used as cord.

Barren Grounds The treeless plains of northern Canada located to the west of Hudson Bay.

bushmen Any of the various types of humans and near-humans believed by the Chipewyans to lurk in the woods and cause mischief.

caribou A subspecies of reindeer that ranges in northern North America and Siberia.

Cree An Algonquin tribe that inhabited the area to the south and east of the Chipewyans.

culture The learned behavior of humans; nonbiological, socially taught activities; the way of life of a group of people.

culture heroes Admirable characters in Chipewyan mythology who demonstrate self-reliance and skillful hunting ability.

Dene Nation A group of Native Americans in northern Canada seeking greater autonomy and territorial protection for its members.

dogiques Chipewyan Roman Catholics who ensured that other Chipewyans adhered to church rules but who lacked power within the Catholic religious hierarchy.

Dogrib An Athapaskan tribe that inhabited an area west of the Chipewyans.

factories In northern Canada, the trading posts of the Hudson's Bay Company.

home guard A group of Native American hunters hired by a factory to provide the traders with game.

Hudson's Bay Company A fur-trading company that controlled a large part of what is now Canada from 1670 to 1870.

inkonze Literally, "to know a little something." Inkonze is magical knowledge used to aid hunting, divine the future, and heal the sick.

Inuit Also known as Eskimos, a tribe that occupied the tundra area to the north of the Chipewyans.

made beaver Originally a pelt from an adult beaver in good condition, made beaver became a sort of currency used by fur traders in the Canadian north.

Métis A person of mixed Native American and European descent.

Northern Indians A group of Chipewyans living directly west of Hudson Bay at the time of the arrival of Europeans into Canada.

Northwest Passage A feasible trade route around the northern end of the American continent that was sought for and never found by various European explorers.

Oblates Members of the Roman Catholic Oblate Order of Mary Immaculate, which was founded in southern France in 1814. The Oblates came into contact with the Chipewyans in 1845.

Statement of the Government of Canada on Indian Policy A government publication printed for the information of Parliament in 1969 that suggested that Canada should abolish the special legal status of its indigenous population.

taboo A ritual restriction on a person's behavior intended to protect them from supernatural harm.

treaty Indians Also known as status Indians, members of tribes who signed treaties with the Canadian government granting Canada sovereignty over their territory in exchange for special benefits and legal protections.

tribe A society consisting of several separate communities united by kinship, culture, language, and other social institutions, including clans and religious organizations.

wife wrestling A hair- and ear-pulling contest held between two men when one wishes to take the other's wife.

Yellowknives Also called the Copper Indians, a group of Chipewyans who lived between the Great Slave and Contwoyto lakes at the time of the arrival of Europeans into Canada. They were wiped out by a combination of disease and warfare in the early 1820s.

INDEX

PICTURE CREDITS

Illustration by Franklin Arbuckle, Picture Collection, P-417(N8263), Hudson's Bay Company Archives, Provincial Archives of Manitoba: p. 60; Photo by Campbell & Chipman, 1987/363-M-39/4(N11860), Hudson's Bay Company Archives, Provincial Archives of Manitoba: p. 71; Canadian Museum of Civilization, Geological Survey of Canada Collection 74880: p. 25; © 1990 Valerie A. Conrad, Government of the Northwest Territories Archives: pp. 86, 93, 94; Glenbow Archives, Calgary, Alberta: pp. 12, 22 (NA-3248-10), 30 (NA-513-5), 64 (NA-3548-1), 73 (NA-4624-1), 76 (NA-3394-38); Government of the Northwest Territories Archives, C. W. Mathers/NWT Archives, N79-058:0012: p. 84; Government of the Northwest Territories Archives, Lorne Smith/NWT Archives, N91-028:0122: p. 91; Haffenreffer Museum of Anthropology, Brown University: cover, pp. 50, 52, 54, 55, 56; Photo by Richard Harrington, Hudson's Bay Company Archives, Provincial Archives of Manitoba: pp. 32 (1987/363-C-14A/44 [N11911]), 35 (1987/363-I-71/15 [N1222]), 40 (1987/363-C-14A/8 [N11910]); Illustration by A. H. Hider, Hudson's Bay Company Archives, Provincial Archives of Manitoba, Picture Collection P-386 (N7565): p. 65; Hudson's Bay Company Archives, Provincial Archives of Manitoba: pp. 47 (OL 737.R632m3p.125 [N8318]), 66 (FC3212.2H4 [N7926]); Drawing by James Isham, Hudson's Bay Company Archives, Provincial Archives of Manitoba: p. 57; National Archives of Canada: pp. 17 (Neg. no. PA101120), 20 (Neg. no. C94110), 37 (Neg. no. PA48097), 44 (Neg. no. C16758), 58 (Neg. no. C73431), 75 (Neg. no. C128029), 81 (Neg. no. C43198), 89 (Neg. no. C38173); National Museum of Denmark, Ethnology Department: pp. 19 (H1:24), 28 (H1:44); Provincial Archives of Alberta Photograph Collection B5461: p. 83; Courtesy of the Provincial Archives of Manitoba: pp. 14–15; Courtesy of the Provincial Museum of Alberta, Edmonton, Alberta: pp. 49 (Cat. #H64.12.3), 51 (Cat. #H66.233.138); Courtesy of the Provincial Museum of Alberta, Edmonton, Alberta, Collection of the Missionary Oblates-Grandin Province des Missionnaires Oblats-Province Grandin: p. 53 (Cat. #H62.2.257a/b); Photo by Coke Smyth, Picture Collection, P-43 (N5255), Hudson's Bay Company Archives, Provincial Archives of Manitoba: p. 68; A. V. Thomas Collection 126, N8200, Courtesy of the Provincial Archives of Manitoba: p. 78; Photo by J. B. Tyrrell, Hudson's Bay Company Archives, Provincial Archives of Manitoba: p. 42 (1987/363-I [N53A154]).

Map (p. 2) by Gary Tong.

KIM DRAMER has a Ph.D. in history from Columbia University in New York City. She has written several books on Native American culture and world history, and her articles have appeared in numerous publications, including the *New York Times,* the New York *Daily News, Ovation* magazine, and *Opera Canada* magazine.

FRANK W. PORTER III, general editor of INDIANS OF NORTH AMERICA, is director of the Chelsea House Foundation for American Indian Studies. He holds a B.A., M.A., and Ph.D. from the University of Maryland. He has done extensive research concerning the Indians of Maryland and Delaware and is the author of numerous articles on their history, archaeology, geography, and ethnography. He was formerly director of the Maryland Commission on Indian Affairs and American Indian Research and Resource Institute, Gettysburg, Pennsylvania, and he has received grants from the Delaware Humanities Forum, the Maryland Committee for the Humanities, the Ford Foundation, and the National Endowment for the Humanities, among others. Dr. Porter is the author of *The Bureau of Indian Affairs* in the Chelsea House KNOW YOUR GOVERNMENT series.